FROM TESTS
TO THERAPY

FROM TESTS TO THERAPY

A PERSONAL HISTORY OF CLINICAL PSYCHOLOGY

G. ALAN SMITH

Matador
5 Weir Road
Kibworth Beauchamp
Leicester LE8 0LQ, UK
Tel: (+44) 116 279 2299
Fax: (+44) 116 279 2277
Email: books@troubador.co.uk
Web: www.troubador.co.uk/matador

ISBN 978 1848765 221

British Library Cataloguing in Publication Data.
A catalogue record for this book is available from the British Library.

Typeset in 11pt Palatino by Troubador Publishing Ltd, Leicester, UK
Printed and bound in Great Britain by TJI Digital, Padstow, Cornwall

Matador is an imprint of Troubador Publishing Ltd

To all my patients

CONTENTS

INTRODUCTION

The young and modern profession of clinical psychology began, like other exciting things, in the 1960s. It had been brewing since the beginning of the century, with ingredients from academic experimental psychology, and added flavours from popular or self-help psychology. Other authors (1) have described the steady development of clinical theories and practice, with influences from various parts of the world, particularly the USA.

A unique feature of British clinical psychology has been its relationship with the National Health Service, which has been both a vital support and a challenging constraint. By being part of a state-funded organisation, clinical psychology has been largely sheltered from the day-to-day market forces that operate in private practice. This has enabled it to serve a broader range of clients, whether rich or poor, without any need to consider the financial implications for the individual patient. The NHS has also generously supported activities such as professional training, research and teaching, which are an essential part of a psychologist's role but which may be neglected if time and money are not available.

The downside of the NHS, of course, is that there is a huge demand for its services, because it is free. This is what it's all about, of course, but there is always the danger of our small profession becoming totally overwhelmed by a need to meet these demands. However, this pressure could be seen as a positive incentive to develop new ideas, as well as to claim more resources.

The other challenging aspect of the NHS is that it is a vast organisation, covering many different trades and professions. There are multiple rivalries between all these groups, sometimes becoming acute, bitter and time-consuming. Boundary disputes may arise out of overlapping skills and functions. Situations may also be set alight by professional self-importance and social class prejudices. The NHS sometimes becomes a startling caricature of the British social class system. Clinical psychologists have found themselves squeezed uncomfortably between the 'upper class' of the medical profession, and a 'lower class' (the rest of the health service staff). As a young and vulnerable group, psychologists have had to struggle to establish their own independent position.

In amongst all that, the NHS has a vast and creaking bureaucracy, which has been in a state of turmoil for many years due to shifts in government policy. Psychologists (and most others) have been very vexed by all this, but sometimes they have managed to take advantage of any fleeting policies that might have had some merit. A few psychologists have even taken the opportunity to move into managerial positions.

The profession has been very successful in several ways. Its numbers have increased steadily and impressively. In 1970 (when I was starting) there were 362 members of the Clinical Division of the British Psychological Society, increasing to 2982 in 1996. By 2009 this has risen to 8134. Not all of them are 'working clinical psychologists', so the figures cannot be taken too literally, but they do show a considerable expansion over this time.

And we have always punched above our weight, even when our numbers were tiny. We had the advantage of being highly educated and articulate, not to mention the fact that many of us were on a mission. Psychology wasn't just a good career (although it was that as well). We wanted to change things and drag the treatment of mental illness into the present century. Indeed there has been much progress, but there is still a great deal left to do.

Instead of writing a dryly academic history of British clinical psychology, I have preferred to record my own personal experiences of working during the period from 1969 to 2000. Now that the profession is better established (although some might still dispute that), it is understandable if our younger colleagues have forgotten (or never knew) what we had to go through, to get to where they are now. Perhaps it is better indeed to forget the blood, sweat and tears. But the past is history and could easily repeat itself.

I have written the book partly in diary form, in order to indicate my thoughts and feelings *at the time*. These are not necessarily what I think and feel today, now that I have greater knowledge, hindsight and emotional distance. Alongside the diary there are italicised sections which are a commentary on the diary, including background information (some of which I did not know at the time) and any relevant subsequent developments.

The beginning was the Maudsley training course in London, where I learned about enlightened and scientific approaches to mental illness. In the later stages of that course I took a step back into the previous century at a Victorian asylum in Canterbury, which demonstrated very clearly what we were up against. Undeterred, I moved on to rural Worcestershire, to a rather nicer Victorian asylum, in order to set up my own psychology department. I was expected to carry out psychological tests, and occasionally I would be allowed to try out a little of the new behaviour therapy.

Worcester then acquired the first of the new psychiatric hospitals, which would lead the way towards the closure of all the Victorian asylums. Now that the modern age of community services had started, I wanted to make psychologists and psychological therapy more accessible, through General Practitioners and not exclusively through Psychiatrists. But the Psychiatrists decided to stand in our way, and moving them aside became a long and painful battle.

After gaining my independence from the psychiatrists, life became a marathon series of patients requiring therapy for anxiety, depression, obsessions, addictions, and indeed all manner of problems. For many years this task was extremely satisfying and absorbing, but gradually it became an unrelenting treadmill. Eventually retirement became a welcome option.

In this book, I have mentioned very little about my psychologist colleagues. Their numbers gradually increased over the years, and they specialised in other tasks with other sorts of patients. I cannot tell their stories for them. Suffice it to say that their support was very much appreciated and has not been forgotten.

I have also deliberately excluded much about my personal life during this time, except for those events which had a clear effect on my professional work, or which were related to it.

THE MAUDSLEY

The Maudsley Hospital in Denmark Hill, Camberwell, South London is unique as a psychiatric hospital. It was conceived in 1907, and was intended to be a liberation from the traditions of the old Victorian lunatic asylums (2).

Originally, of course, the old asylums were meant to provide a more humane type of care for the mentally ill, compared with the previous strategy of regarding them as hopeless creatures who needed to be locked up. Unfortunately the Victorian laws on lunacy required patients to be certified, a legal process that was difficult to reverse, with the result that many patients remained in the asylum even if they were no longer ill. However, apparently there was an escape clause (!) that if a patient managed to run away and hide for two weeks, the law allowed them to remain free.

The Maudsley opened in 1923, and was intended to be a centre for treatment and research rather than confinement and asylum. A specific Act of Parliament had to be obtained to allow the hospital to accept voluntary patients, who could come and go according to their needs. The hospital was exclusively for early and acute cases, had out-patients, and encouraged research to discover more effective treatments. Training courses were provided to improve the psychiatric skills of medical and nursing staff. Gradually and eventually the old asylums (which remained open until the seventies and eighties) tried to follow the example of the Maudsley, but never quite succeeded.

Next door to the Maudsley Hospital is the Institute of Psychiatry building, which opened in 1967 to house the previous Maudsley Medical School, as well as other research specialities related to mental health problems. There is a department of Psychology, led from 1955 to 1983 by Professor Hans Eysenck. There is also a postgraduate course for the training of Clinical Psychologists, led by Monte Shapiro from its modest beginnings in 1947 until 1974.

5th October 1969.

I'm on the Maudsley course! How I got here is a bit of a mystery, and I can't believe my luck. People tell me that this is the elite clinical psychology training course, *the* place to be. I feel a bit of a fraud, but I think I have worked out the chain of events which led to me being accepted.

As a working class lad in the industrial North East of England, I had sent myself south to Exeter University because it was a long way from home and there were green fields, blue sea views and sunshine. Nearing the end of that course, for the basic psychology degree, I really didn't know where to go next.

But then one of the lecturers gave me an application form for the Maudsley MPhil course, and I sent it in. Now it so happened that the Maudsley psychologists at this time had adopted a bravely principled scientific approach to student applications. They had decided not to carry out interviews any more, as interviewing was clearly an unscientific procedure, full of irrelevant social and psychological prejudices. Instead they were going to base their decisions solely upon the applicant's examination results.

However, at this stage our degree results were not yet available, which was just as well, as I had spent too much time gazing at the blue sea views and too little time at lectures.

Instead, they used our last known results, namely the GCE A-level exams taken at school. And I had quite a few top marks, mainly in Mathematics. Perhaps they thought that a mathematician would make a good scientific psychologist. So by return of post I was offered a place on the Maudsley course.

The only snag was money. There were a limited number of student grants available, but these would go to those with the best grades in their degrees. I already expected that I would not be one of them. Fortunately, there were funds for three students out of National Health Service money, for those who intended to take up jobs in the NHS after qualifying. Unlike the scientists at the Maudsley, the Health Service still carried out interviews, and fortunately I was able to assure them that I was enthusiastic about becoming an NHS psychologist.

So not only am I on the Maudsley course, I am already an NHS employee. And unlike most of the other students (who are on grants), I feel quite well-paid. The salary of an NHS student psychologist is about the same as my dad's earnings as a plumber! That has really impressed my mother, who had scoffed at the idea that anyone could earn a living out of something as airy fairy as Psychology.

13th October 1969.

I sat next to Eysenck in the canteen today! Normally I would never have dared to plonk myself down alongside the great Professor, but the canteen was full and this was the only empty chair. I was wandering round with my tray, and hesitated by this space for just a second before I realised that it would have looked insulting not to sit down. Eysenck was very civil about it, and simply said Hi before carrying on conversing with his colleagues. *Wow, I'm sitting next to Eysenck!* These were the words that kept going through my mind. It was a bit like finding yourself standing next to Freud in the gents' toilets.

Hans Eysenck is of course one of the really big names of psychology. But more importantly for me he was the trigger for my decision to take it up as a career. I have read that Eysenck was born in Berlin, but left Germany in the 1930s to come to England because of his opposition to the Nazis. From the 1950s onwards he wrote prolifically about psychology as a science, and has had a huge influence in Britain and indeed the whole world.

It was in 1963 that I came across one of his books in Gateshead public library, next door to the Grammar School. At that time I was doing my Mathematics and Physics A-levels, but growing increasingly bored with repetitive calculations. As a teenager I often browsed around the public library hoping to find secret knowledge about life, and I had worked my way through most of the literary fiction.

So one day I did something different and ventured down an unknown set of shelves in a rather dark corner. I was glad it was hidden away where the librarians could not watch me, as it was strangely embarrassing to be looking at these books. No, they weren't about sex, they were about psychology. There was a short row of books, about half a dozen, and they stood next to the much larger Witchcraft section (*much the same happens today, except that Witchcraft has become Mind, Body, and Spirit*).

Most of the psychology books were based upon the psychoanalytic ideas of Freud and Jung. Very entertaining, but Eysenck would have regarded them as no better than the neighbouring witchcraft books. My eye was caught by the one book on the shelf written by him (3). This book had numbers in it, rather than the usual literary style of psychoanalysis. It described how to do experiments that would support or disprove your theories, rather than simply accepting the ideas of higher authority or just making it up. It showed that psychology could (and should) be a science. This appealed to me greatly, especially the idea of getting into something quite new.

When I sat next to Eysenck in the canteen today, I thought of all this, but kept my mouth shut. It is difficult to tell someone that they are responsible for you being where you are.

20th October 1969.

We had an arithmetic test today! One thing you have to study as a psychologist, at least if you want to be a scientific one, is Mathematical Statistics. How else could you work out the results of group experiments or surveys, or look for patterns amongst otherwise random behaviours? But I was amazed that only three of us passed this preliminary test in simple arithmetic. It was easy for me, having done all that maths at school and university, but how will the rest of them ever learn to do more advanced statistical calculations? Perhaps they can always get someone else to do the maths for you, such as that friendly statistician down the corridor. I hope it is not a sign that the new scientific psychologists have feet of clay.

27th October 1969.

Great shock today! Monte Shapiro decided to rid us of the last of our illusions, and gave us a lecture in which he announced that neither he nor any of the other psychologists at the Maudsley knew how to treat patients effectively (4). And therefore they would not be teaching us how to do therapy. If we wanted to become therapists we would have to find our own way.

That is what his words said, but somehow his manner tells another story. Monte Shapiro seems a very kindly man, unassuming and happy to listen, even to inexperienced students such as ourselves. That sort of style would be an excellent starting point for treating patients, I think.

I know what he means, though. The Maudsley is in the process of doing research that has shown an encouraging degree of effectiveness when certain methods (Behaviour Therapy) are used for treating certain problems (Phobias). But if a patient comes along with another problem of a kind not yet studied, then we will be in scientifically unexplored territory. We would have to set up some kind of exploratory experiment and see if we learned anything.

10th November 1969.

I had a successful day today, doing my *pass out*. This strange bit of Maudsley jargon refers to being watched by your tutor while doing an IQ test on a patient, in order to assess whether you have learned how to do it properly. It is funny that they use that phrase, as if you were a military cadet now becoming a qualified officer! There is indeed some parallel with that, because when you are an officially approved IQ tester, the world recognises you as a real psychologist. One of my mother's favourite insults about people was that *they should go and get their brains tested.* And here I am now, a certified brains tester!

Only psychologists are allowed to give proper IQ tests. Not even psychiatrists can do this (not that they would want to). Psychiatrists tolerate the existence of our upstart profession by regarding clinical psychologists as junior technical assistants. A psychologist is employed to do IQ tests on any patient selected by the psychiatrist. At least that is what they think, and we are obliged to humour them.

Actually, I rather like giving IQ tests, even when there is no useful result. It is one way of becoming accustomed to seeing patients, desensitising myself to the anxiety of this novel situation. There's a set routine and a clear purpose to the session, but at the same time there is still room for a chat. We use the WAIS (the Wechsler Adult Intelligence Scale) or the similar WISC for children. It isn't one of those forms that the person fills in on their own, but rather the tester goes through each item individually with the patient. You have to stick to a precise order of doing things, and of course you must give no clue to the answers. But you can give general encouragement and reassurance to the patient, to give them the best chance of showing their true abilities.

There are several subtests measuring Verbal abilities, and several more to assess visuospatial skills (Performance IQ). So you get two main scores or IQs, and normally they are about the same, within about 10 points or so. But some people score quite differently on these two IQs. They are significantly better at verbal skills than visuospatial ones, or vice versa. This can be simply a normal variant, but you might have to discuss whether the patient's job matches his skills. However, sometimes a discrepancy between IQs can be the result of mental illness (which causes a loss of concentration or motivation), or even a physical brain impairment such as dementia, neurological diseases, tumours or strokes.

Using a set of IQ tests to look for these kinds of clues can be very interesting, and occasionally even exciting when you find something that no one else had spotted. Sometimes you can be the bearer of good news, such as when you find that a person has a much higher IQ than they had ever realised. This can raise not only a smile, but also some thoughts about achieving a different path in life.

17th November 1969.

I've been seconded to the Neurosurgical Department. I'm glad to hear that I won't have to watch a brain operation, although my tutor says that she has done so. This experience is not on offer for lowly student psychologists. My job here is to test patients before and after they have had brain surgery. As well as the IQ tests, I have to learn how to do a set of memory tests, measuring verbal and also visual memory, using immediate recall and also recall after a delay and interruption.

My supervisor is interested in whether these tests can give any useful indication of where the patient's brain problem lies. If there is a tumour deep inside the left hand side of the brain, it will impair the IQ and memory tests differently to when it is in the right hand side of the brain. And the effects will be different again if the damage is on the surface of the brain, as opposed to the interior. However, she has warned me not to try telling the brain surgeon where the problem is. Our tests can be misleading in that respect, and indeed sometimes give no clue whatsoever. The surgeons prefer to rely on their own judgement based upon their clinical neurological tests and X-rays (*this was before the era of MRI or CT scans*).

So why do they want psychological tests done? My supervisor explained that in brain surgery there is always a risk of doing damage. Either accidentally or through necessity, the surgeon might destroy some vital part. The patient's life might be saved, but at the expense of his brain power. Our tests are a way of reassuring everyone that the patient is no worse after the operation, and indeed sometimes considerably better. If unfortunately the patient's IQ and memory has suffered a decline, then we can provide evidence as to how much.

As a warning about the sometimes unpredictable nature of brain functioning, my supervisor told me about a man who had a large tumour and a considerable proportion of his brain had to be removed in the process of saving his life. The psychological tests showed no change. I am not sure if this is true or just a good story!

24th November 1969.

The things that happen when you are trying to concentrate on testing a patient!

There was a young woman this morning, seventeen years old, all bright and cheerful because she had been free of epileptic fits for the past month. She had developed epilepsy in childhood, and it had grown worse and worse until she was having several fits every day. Electroencephalographic (EEG) tests had discovered that her seizures were fired up from one small area of the brain, and she agreed that the surgeons could remove this area in the hope that the rest of the brain would then behave itself.

When I saw her this morning to check out her IQ and memory functioning, she was thrilled to have got her life back. She had celebrated by going out and getting some tattoos, which seemed a bit strange to me but I said nothing. I know that tattoos are quite normal for some people.

'Would you like to see them?' she asked, and it would have been unkind to refuse. She hoisted up her miniskirt to expose some blue and yellow floral briefs and a pair of ample thighs, upon which there was some writing in black ink. One thigh said HOPE, and the other said FEAR. I hope I didn't look too astonished. 'Very nice', I managed to say. Her test results proved to be quite normal, by the way.

Then this afternoon I was testing a young man who had been admitted for surgery for a brain tumour. He did not look at all well, and he warned me that he was struggling with a feeling of nausea. His tumour was in the front part of his brain, so I had been told to carry out a test (the Wisconsin Card Sorting Test) which can be particularly affected by damage in that area. The test involves getting the person to sort a series of cards according to colour or shape or size, and he has to guess which of these features you have chosen. You simply tell him Right or Wrong, and after some trial and error he works out that you want him to sort according to colour, for example. But then you move the goal posts, *without telling him,* and choose another feature such as shape. When you start telling him Wrong, he has to first realise that you have changed tack, and then he works out by trial and error again that you want him to sort by shape.

I must admit that I feel uncomfortable with the idea of moving the goalposts in such an underhand manner. This is an important part of the test, to see how long the person will persist with his first solution. But it feels really mean, and almost cruel. You can see the patient being knocked back and confused. With this young man today, I had just moved the goalposts for the first time and suddenly he vomited, all over the cards! This has made me very wary of using that test again.

10th March 1970.

There are a huge number of agoraphobics in London. I've been busy trying to treat a few of them. The Maudsley has the right idea, I am sure, in treating this problem by behavioural methods. Instead of trying to find some hopelessly elusive cause in the patient's childhood or unconscious mind, why not get straight to the point and give down-to-earth assistance in overcoming their fear?

We have been given some instruction and training in the principles and techniques of desensitisation or gradual exposure. The patient has to face his fear, but he is more likely to do this successfully if he advances just one step at a time. And you have to remember that each phobia is actually two fears. An agoraphobic is not only nervous of being out in a public place, he is also afraid of these anxiety feelings. He fears that he might collapse or go mad, or somehow make a fool of himself.

So first we take the patient through a progressive relaxation training procedure, which is intended to show him that he can exert some degree of control over his physical anxiety, and therefore he can be less fearful of it. Simply learning to breathe very slowly is a good way of limiting a panic attack. In the clinic the patient sits in a comfortable easy chair, and we tell him to close his eyes. Then we get him to tense up each part of his body in turn, and then to relax it. We go through each part of the body in turn, taking about fifteen minutes in total, and part of the technique is for the therapist to adopt a very soothing and rhythmic style of speech.

Some patients comment that it is like being sent to sleep, and others ask if it is the same as hypnosis. Actually, it isn't a million miles from hypnosis, and some patients say they feel as if they are floating up to the ceiling! But we are keen to dispel this notion. As scientists we scorn unproven practices, and as behaviourists we want our patients to improve through active learning and not passively through magic tricks.

The next stage is to get the patient to sit relaxed and imagine that he is in some feared situation (going into a shop, perhaps).

Just imagining this scene will usually make him feel some tension even while sitting safely in his chair, and he is then talked into relaxing again. This process is repeated hundreds of times over several weekly sessions, building it up until he can imagine doing things that he could never imagine before.

At some point the patient then needs to be persuaded to try going out into these actual situations, again in a step-by-step sort of way. One way of encouraging a patient is to go with them. This enables you to push them into making the effort, but at the same time they are reassured that you are there to rescue them if necessary.

Doing this therapy has given me a novel way of seeing London through the eyes of agoraphobics. Perhaps the tourist board ought to run Phobic Tours! On to Tube trains, and off at the next station before too much panic sets in. Up and down escalators repeatedly until anxiety has worn off. Up and down in lifts again and again until it gets really boring (or the lift breaks down!). In and out of shops with no intention of buying anything, just wandering with an eye on the exit.

It is quite hard work, all this. You are out on your own with someone for whom you feel responsible, someone who might panic at any moment, and you have to try to look calm and confident to reassure them. Fortunately, there hasn't been any great problem (so far!), except this morning, and that was for another reason. I have been given the task of escorting an agoraphobic lady in the mornings when she comes to the Day Hospital. She lives only a quarter of a mile away, but such a journey makes her extremely anxious, and she has been stuck at home for quite a long time. She can't imagine getting on the bus yet, but she has agreed to try walking with someone to the hospital.

They warned me that she lives on the twelfth floor of a block of flats, but she is OK with the lift. Unfortunately when I got there this morning, the lift was out of order. There was no choice but to climb up the stairs, upwards and onwards until I was completely out of breath. She told me that the lift is often out of order, but it would be fixed by this afternoon.

Coming down the stairs was easy, of course. When she got to the street, she started to look tense and shaky, and half way up the road she was looking as if she too had climbed up twelve floors. But onwards we walked, and at the hospital she heaved a sigh of relief.

5th May 1970.

I've been sent to Bethlem Royal Hospital on attachment for a few months. This is a mainstream mental hospital in Bromley, South London, in the same group as the Maudsley. Everyone makes the same joke about being sent to Bedlam, and I am no exception.

The original Bethlem or Bethlehem Hospital (5) dates back to the 1300s, located in the City of London until it moved to Southwark in 1815, and then to the present site in 1930. By the 1600s the hospital was notorious for the brutal treatment handed out to its inmates. The word **bedlam***, meaning uproar and confusion, is derived from its name. In the 1700s people used to go to Bedlam to stare at the lunatics, as if it were a zoo. Even worse, they were allowed to poke the inmates with long sticks. However, in modern times Bethlem Royal has been at an advantage compared with the old Victorian asylums, in having a more modern building together with its connection with the Maudsley.*

12th May 1970.

I'm doing some time in the drug addiction unit at the Royal

Bethlem. We aren't allowed to get involved in their treatment, but my supervisor is running some research to try to find ways of assessing progress, such as measuring their degree of craving for heroin. The addicts are going through cold turkey, i.e. total withdrawal of their drugs, and I must say that I was quite shaken by my first sight of this. Dishevelled and pale young men in dressing gowns were pacing up and down, focussed on their loss and smoking heavily. The door was locked. They had agreed to that.

My supervisor took from his pocket a small bottle of heroin tablets obtained from the hospital pharmacist. They were very small white tablets, and we placed one in front of each recovering addict, who tried to assess how much he craved it today. In order to put a figure on the strength of his craving, the question was *How much money would you pay for this heroin right now?* Some of them named extraordinary amounts, such as tens of thousands of pounds. I am not sure whether this tells us more about their attitude to the question, or at least their attitude to money, than it tells us about the strength of their craving.

19th May 1970.

It has been a warm sunny spring day, and the gardens at Bethlem Royal are a joy. There are dozens of large rhododendrons lining the driveway into the hospital, and they are out in flower. I haven't seen anything like it in any other hospital grounds. After nearly a year in South London, it has been a pleasurable escape to travel on the bus out to Bethlem Royal. It isn't exactly the countryside, but you can start to feel that green fields might be somewhere within reach. I'm beginning to feel tired of the concrete and traffic noise of London.

2

ST. AUGUSTINE'S

The Kent County Asylum was St. Augustine's Hospital, just a few miles south-west of Canterbury. Opened in 1875, it eventually closed in 1992, having been replaced by community based services. It was in the usual style of red brick with grey slate roofs, with a clock tower and water tower. Like many of the Victorian asylums, it was known locally by the name of its nearest village, Chartham.

8th September 1970.

The price of being on a Health Service salary is that I have to spend the second year of my training course at an ordinary mental hospital in the Kent region. Every Thursday I travel back to the Maudsley for lectures. My fellow students on grants are staying on at the Maudsley, and feel that they are on the better option, having heard daunting tales about life at the old mental hospitals. However, I am simply glad to be out of London, on my way to wherever my career takes me.

I have already decided that eventually I want to live in a small but interesting town within sight of the countryside, rather than a big city. My supervisors offered me a choice of three hospitals in Kent, recommending two of them because they thought well of the psychologists there. The third option was Canterbury, further away and uncertain in quality. So naturally I have chosen Canterbury, a place that was often mentioned in my history lessons at school in County Durham. I am still being a tourist. Why go to Maidstone when you can go to Canterbury?

This morning I met John, the Senior Psychologist at St. Augustine's. He is obviously pleased that those important psychologists in London have blessed him by sending a student for the first time, but clearly he is wary about this intrusion of the Maudsley into the world of St. Augustine's. He warns me that I am still young and naive, and that *swallowing the Maudsley line* will be a great handicap in the real world of real mental hospitals.

I nodded politely to reassure him, as I do have some inkling of what he means. But I am not sure yet whether he has any better ideas for dealing with mental illness, or whether he is simply concerned with surviving in his job and not rocking the boat. I am not impressed with his confession that his only academic qualification is in theology. He is quite old now, and in his day the NHS had no idea what a psychologist was, let alone what qualifications they should have.

Maybe it is significant that he has nine children, which might indicate a certain resistance to ideas of the modern age, such as family planning. And of course a need to hang on to his job to support his family. He has already mentioned his resentment that the hospital authorities have refused to promote him from Senior to Principal psychologist. His colleagues in the other Kent hospitals have all received this upgrade, because they have better connections with the Maudsley, he thinks.

15th September 1970.

Already I am being a nuisance to John. I have refused to test patients with the MMPI diagnostic questionnaire, because the Maudsley tells me that it is rubbish. He says I must do what I think best, but I can tell that I have stood on lots of toes, and not just his.

The Maudsley's objection to the MMPI is that the science behind it is flawed. Eysenck is busy developing his own purer forms of personality test, backed by experimental data. My own objection to the MMPI is that it is illogical to apply it to patients in order to get a psychiatric diagnosis. Why give a patient a form to fill in when they have already been questioned by a psychiatrist? Aren't these psychiatrists doing their job?

Also it simply doesn't feel right. The MMPI is amazingly long and tedious, and some of the questions appear to be stupid or even offensive. Patients come to see John, and they sit in the waiting room for an hour filling in this form before he speaks to them. I can't believe that this is a good introduction to seeing a psychologist. But I cannot say this to John. He thinks he is being very scientific, as the MMPI test results come in the form of a very impressive graph.

There have been other awkward moments. The psychiatrist who asked me to give an MMPI to one of his in-patients was astounded when I refused. This went to the heart of the relationship between psychiatrists and psychologists. What was the point of having a psychologist around the place if they wouldn't do what they were asked? The psychiatrist was wondering whether he had diagnosed this patient correctly, so I offered to interview the patient and give a second opinion. But no, a psychologist isn't qualified to do this, not being a psychiatrist. A psychologist is qualified only to carry out tests, but not to choose which tests to do, nor to question their usefulness. This is the real world away from the Maudsley.

The MMPI (Minnesota Multiphasic Personality Inventory) is a long questionnaire with nearly 600 questions, taking the patient over an hour to complete. It gives score patterns which suggest a psychiatric diagnosis for the patient: Hypochondriasis, Depression, Hysteria,

Psychopathy, Paranoia, Neurosis, Schizophrenia, Hypomania, and so on. The questions and scores were based upon patients who had been clearly diagnosed (by psychiatrists) as having these disorders.

The idea of having a questionnaire was that anyone could be assessed for mental illness without necessarily seeing a psychiatrist. Indeed the MMPI was applied to the screening of many thousands of American military recruits for the Second World War, when it would not have been possible for psychiatrists to interview them all. It has had to be considerably revised, and is now done on a computer screen rather than on a paper form, but it still takes a long time. Many psychologists and psychiatrists (especially in the USA) are very enthusiastic about the MMPI, but equally many others still consider it highly dubious (6).

22nd September 1970.

I have to find a solution to this. I can't just go round saying that the Maudsley has declared all these things to be unscientific rubbish. A compromise is needed. The psychiatrists are permitting us to see some of their patients, but only on condition that we carry out testing. And from our own professional point of view, surely we need to see some of their patients. We need to expand our knowledge and experience of the whole range of mental illnesses. Maybe we can actually think of something useful to do with them. Or maybe at least we can keep an eye on what the psychiatrists are doing. No one else is in a position to do that.

29th September 1970.

I have a solution! I will use any tests that the Maudsley agree to be valid and reliable, namely the WAIS IQ, and some memory tests. These tests might not be relevant to the question being asked, but at least they are an accurate measure of intellectual performance! If the psychiatrist wants to know if a patient's illness is a psychosis such as schizophrenia, I can go along to the ward with my box of tricks, looking like an expert, and I can watch and listen to the patient while he is doing these tests. If he scores a low or high IQ, or good or poor memory, this may (or may not) tell us something about his clinical state, or at least his level of concentration. At the same time, I can have a chat to him, asking questions to see if I get any answers that differ from those gathered by the psychiatrist. If nothing else, I will actually learn something myself from the experience. A set of MMPI scores from a form would have told me nothing.

And it keeps the psychiatrists reasonably happy! Now that they have got over the shock of having a psychologist who does things differently to John (who is just about the only psychologist they had ever met), they don't actually mind too much. I can see now that keeping the psychiatrists happy is an unavoidable consideration at the present stage in the development of our profession. At the Maudsley we are protected from the psychiatric view of things, because our supervisors deal with all that. At the Maudsley Day Hospital I had become aware of the possibility that a paranoid patient might be formulating plans to kill me, but now at St. Augustine's I have also discovered a need to watch my back against psychiatrists!

6th October 1970.

Actually, these psychiatrists are as fascinating as the patients. They are masters of the art of maintaining their position even when the tide is running against them. For example, there is the quiet battle of the dining room.

At lunch today John explained the mysterious rules of the hospital dining room.

Cooked meals are provided for the staff of St. Augustine's at a generously small charge, this being one of the perks of a hospital job. The canteen is located in a very large room which looks as though it used to be a ballroom. There is a raised stage at one end populated by the ghosts of Victorian musicians and actors. The ballroom floor is now home to dozens of small plastic canteen tables, at which are seated little groups of nurses both male and female, a few porters and domestics, and now one or two psychologists and an occasional occupational therapist.

But the really weird thing is the long table situated underneath the front of the stage. Only a stately home or a lunatic asylum would have a table as big as that. It is covered with white linen, and laid with best cutlery. When I noticed it last week there was no one at this table, and I thought that perhaps it was being prepared for some formal occasion. But today there was a man sitting there eating in splendid isolation, and I asked John who he was. I learned that this was one of the Consultant Psychiatrists, and this is the Doctors' Table.

But actually no, it is no longer the Doctors' Table. It is now called the Waitress Service Table. A small social revolution has taken place in the past year, and now all staff, however lowly, are in theory allowed to eat at this table. They just have to pay an extra sixpence for the waitress. A very small sum to avoid the canteen queue. How very democratic! So why does no one sit there except the doctors? All the different birds flock together, but only with their own kind. Nurses sit with nurses at plastic tables, and doctors with doctors at the linen tablecloth. Where do psychologists fit in? At the plastic tables presumably.

That's where I feel comfortable. At the Maudsley, even Professor Eysenck fetches his meal on a tray and eats at a plastic table.

20th October 1970.

I have decided to do an experimental study of delusions for my MPhil thesis, looking at whether you can modify someone's beliefs by changing their behaviour. Where better than a lunatic asylum to study delusions? At least that's what I thought, until I went round the wards asking whether they had any deluded patients. 'You mean like thinking they are Napoleon?' said one charge nurse. 'We haven't got anyone here like that'. This morning they said there is an old lady in one of the long stay wards who thinks she is Queen Victoria, so I went to see her. 'Be careful, she can be a bit aggressive', warned the nurse. Fortunately, old ladies don't move too fast, so when she came after me waving her walking stick, I retreated fairly swiftly. Not quite suitable for my research, I thought.

More luck this afternoon, however. There's a man called Albert Johnson who says that he is a divine being of some sort, with control over the universe. He is allied with God, and his task is to fight Evil, in the form of beings called Them who are trying to destroy the universe. The real Albert was in the army until the age of 20, when he was discharged because of his mental illness. He has wandered Britain, committing petty thefts and stopping at various mental hospitals. He is now 36 and on a locked ward, diagnosed as having chronic paranoid schizophrenia and treated with Largactil. He will do very nicely for my research. I need at least one more patient like this.

27th October 1970.

Albert is a treasure. I just have to set my tape recorder going, and then I ask him to explain who he is, and away he goes:

'Well, my name is Albert, and I was confirmed in Darlington when I was seven. I've never had a good home, because all the time I was travelling with these people called Them. They have always known or suspected that I wasn't who I was. And they used to think, sometimes anyway, that I wasn't Albert. I used to go under various names. I was Ludtec once, I was Licicious, Cranvec and Croner, and Ludnic. My job, when I first got into heaven a long time ago, was .....'

I'm just trying to do something really original for my thesis. None of the other students will have material like this. The idea is first to try to measure how deluded he is, by rating each statement he makes, and then to count how many deluded statements per minute he is coming out with. If I give him some kind of treatment to reduce his delusions, I can measure whether it is having any effect.

The question is: what kind of treatment? It is commonly held that there is no point in debating delusions with the patient, trying to persuade them that they are incorrect (*not true, by the way. That was simply the traditional psychiatric view*). So I am going to give Albert something to do which will be inconsistent with his usual delusional conversation. I am going to get him to pretend to be the unmistakeably human charge nurse on his ward! Only while he is with me, of course. He can tell me a story about his day at work with the patients. Unfortunately, there is a bit of a twist in this tale, as some people joke that this charge nurse also thinks that he is God. I just hope that Albert hasn't heard this rumour.

After talking to me for a while in the manner of the charge nurse, will Albert be any less delusional when I ask him who he really is?

18th November 1970.

On Thursdays I travel up to London for lectures at the Maudsley. That means getting up at 6 am and walking to the railway station. This chore is relieved on these dark mornings by the vision of Canterbury Cathedral in the distance, with soft floodlights making it stand out from the shadows. The stars twinkling above it on a frosty morning pull me forward towards the railway station. By the time I reach London it is daylight and time for coffee.

It was my turn today to give a talk to the lecturers and students, about my project on delusions. Albert is doing quite well, showing some positive results from my treatment, but another patient is not showing any effects whatsoever. The Maudsley people are polite and quite interested, but I can tell that I have strayed from their well-beaten paths. No one else at the Maudsley has done any work on delusions, so it isn't a big topic. Mind you, this means that they don't know much about it, so I can get by with a minimal amount of knowledge.

This isn't the first time that I have discovered the benefit of staying away from the crowd. My decision to become a clinical psychologist hasn't been entirely down to intellectual interest and altruism. I am well aware of the career prospects which arise from the fact that there are only a few hundred clinical psychologists in the whole country, a disproportionate number of them being in or around London. Most of the Maudsley students want to stay in London, and cannot even imagine going elsewhere. When I start applying for a job elsewhere, I should be able to pick and choose. That's quite exciting.

10th February 1971.

There was drama in the St. Augustine's department this morning. John has a second qualified psychologist, a young lady, and she was holding an outpatient clinic. The last patient of the morning was new to her, having been referred by a psychiatrist for assessment of his problems. The referral letter said that this was a young man who wished to have a sex change operation, and did the psychologists think that this was appropriate for him. The young lady psychologist had gone to fetch him from the waiting room, and somehow she had not expected to see a man with short hairy legs in a miniskirt and high heels. Unfortunately, she could not control her shock and fled to the department office to seek help.

The secretary, a glamorous young lady with long smooth legs in a miniskirt and high heels, sprang to the rescue by coming and asking me to see this patient. For some reason, they thought this might be more of a man's job! So I interviewed him, knowing nothing of gender problems nor how to assess them. I just asked him to explain himself, and it all sounded perfectly reasonable, so I have written a report saying so, which should keep everyone happy. The secretary probably did the best assessment by watching him walk down the path away from the department. 'Must get his legs waxed, and needs to learn how to walk on high heels', she said, so I have added this to my report, trying to sound wise about these things.

24th February 1971.

I think I cracked today. Or maybe just saw the light. Every now and again I have been asked to go and see a patient on Ward 6, one of the acute admission wards. This particular ward is a nightmare. You have to be given a bunch of large keys to get into it, and I must admit at first you feel quite important to be carrying the asylum keys. But when you get through the door to Ward 6, you are faced with a scene of distress and panic.

Your possession of the keys makes you a target for distressed and hyped-up patients who think that you are a doctor in authority, and they grasp hold of your arm and plead to be let out. All I can do is to explain that I am not a doctor and have no authority over their situation. They tell me that they hardly ever see a doctor, and I feel ashamed and creep away to the safety of the nurses' office. After chatting to the nurse, I learn that this is not a special secure ward for risky patients, but simply a normal admission ward for short-stay patients. Each ward belongs to one of the four Consultant Psychiatrists, who each cover a specific geographical area of the Canterbury District. If you happen to live in one particular area and become depressed, you would end up in Ward 6. The other wards are not locked and seem much calmer. When I asked the nurse why this ward is different, he shrugged his shoulders. 'It's what Dr. R. wants. We have no say in the matter. Everyone calls him Mad Doctor R. No one seems to be able to do anything about him. He'll probably retire in a few years, so maybe things will change then.'

When I left the ward this morning, I felt angry. I returned to the department and told them that I would refuse to see any more patients on that ward. They said that they were not surprised. Everyone knows about Mad Doctor R. and his locked ward. A group of concerned staff are getting together to try to plot a revolution, but how can anything be changed here?

In 1967 a book called Sans Everything (7) observed that NHS hospitals, and the people who work in them, tended to respond in typical ways to complaints about failures of care. They would deny the problem or dismiss the evidence. Then they laid low and hoped it would go away. They discredited and victimised whistleblowers, implying either malice or excessive zeal.

So it wasn't until 1974 that two members of the nursing staff at St. Augustine's produced a pamphlet called A Critique Regarding Policy, and circulated it internally. After a predictable lack of response from the hospital management, in the following year they produced another pamphlet detailing 70 allegations of nursing malpractice.

This led to the setting up of a Department of Health Enquiry, which published a report in 1976 (8).

The report found gross defects in basic administration, a lack of formal leadership, and a resistance to multidisciplinary working by doctors who resented any reduction in their power. There was a particular mention of the use of ECT (electro-convulsive therapy) as a punishment or threat against non-cooperative patients.

A whole series of such Enquiries took place during the 1970s: Brookwood, Farleigh, Napsbury, Normansfield, Rampton, South Ockendon, etc. They all had similar findings, but the lessons have been learned only slowly. As stated in Sans Everything, the one thing that administrators and committees fail to learn is that kindness, pleasantness, sympathy and forbearance cannot be commanded by giving orders or passing resolutions. These qualities develop (or fail to develop) according to the example of senior staff.

17th March 1971.

I have nearly finished the research for my thesis. My time at St. Augustine's will be over in the summer, thank goodness. It is time to start looking for a job somewhere nice. What a shame I can't stay here. Canterbury is exactly the sort of place I would like to live.

I ought to go back home to the North-East, but I still want to get away from all that grimness. Where do I want to make my new home? I am searching the job adverts and looking at maps at the end of every month.

3

POWICK HOSPITAL

1st September 1971.

I have found where I want to be. Worcestershire is mid-way between North and South, an excellent compromise. I have never visited this part of the world before, but I have an idyllic image of it derived from childhood, listening to the radio serial The Archers, 'An Everyday Story of Country Folk'. But I had a shock when I first got off the train at Worcester Shrub Hill Station and saw a rather grubby set of buildings which did not fit into this image at all. However, things improved as I headed towards Powick Hospital, which is surrounded by green fields half way between Worcester and Malvern.

It was actually the Malvern Hills that made up my mind to take the job. I had an interview with Dr. Arthur Spencer, the Medical Superintendent, who told me how he had unlocked all the wards and given the patients the freedom that they deserved. This at last seemed a humane and relaxed hospital after all the other grim places that I had visited for interview. Had I seen the Malvern Hills, he asked. I had never even heard of them, so he called in one of the assistant psychiatrists to drive me out to the Hills after lunch. This was Dr. Rizvi, a pleasant man in a smart suit and elegant shoes, not really appropriate for a walk up the Hills. Sweating somewhat, we arrived at a point where there was an absolutely magnificent view across the hilly landscape and the Severn valley. That was when I knew that this was the place where I wanted to spend the rest of my life.

I have found myself a little flat in Malvern, and have been doing lots of walking on the Hills during a free week before I start work at the Hospital.

8th September 1971.

It was my first day at Powick today. Dr. Spencer showed me to my department. Not just an office, but a whole suite of three offices, all to myself! Apparently there was one previous psychologist, but he left after only a year. I asked why he left, but got no answer, so I have put a question mark over this. Perhaps he just saw a better job elsewhere.

The offices were in a bit of a shambles, as if the previous occupant had left in a hurry, so I have spent the day just tidying up and getting a desk organised. There is one curious thing, or perhaps two curious things that may or may not be connected. In one of the smaller offices there is a closed circuit TV camera mounted on the wall, connected to controls and a screen in the main office. Always keen on technology, my first reaction is that this could be quite a nice toy to play with, but on the other hand I am not sure what I could actually use it for.

The other thing is more troubling. Inside a big cardboard box I found a square board with metal studs, attached to an electrical wire. This is ringing a bell in my mind. I seem to recall an article in one of the behaviour therapy journals, about aversion therapy for some kind of sexual fetish. That patient was asked to stand on a metal grid in his bare feet, so that he could receive an electric shock while contemplating his bad habit. I had no idea that this kind of therapy might have been carried out in ordinary rural mental hospitals. However, I can find no actual records of what has been going on here. Perhaps I am letting my imagination run away with me.

Upon reflection, I don't like the idea of the CCTV camera. I will take it down and give it back to Dr. Spencer, although he might get upset about having wasted precious hospital funds on this equipment.

9th September 1971.

I had lunch with the psychiatrists today. It proved to be another variant on the theme of medical elitism in hospital dining rooms. Yesterday, in my innocence, I simply went to the canteen, collected my tray of fish pie and apple crumble, and went to sit at one of the plastic tables. I did observe someone carrying their tray and going through a polished wooden door in the corner of the dining room. Perhaps they are taking their lunch into their office, I thought.

But all was revealed today. 'What were you thinking of, yesterday, sitting with the nurses?' asked a nice lady psychiatrist with a grand manner and large blonde hair. 'You must come and sit with us' she said, taking me under her maternal wing. It turns out that the doctors have their own dining room through that door off the main canteen. There is a long wooden table for about eight people, and a sofa to lounge upon afterwards. 'We need this privacy in case we want to discuss patients over lunch', they explained.

So I decided to throw in my lot with the doctors. They did warn me that the nurses might give me black marks for this. 'They are awfully jealous of us having our own dining room, you know'. But I think I have no choice but to try to form some connection with the psychiatrists.

These doctors seem very impressed with me having been to the Maudsley, and don't want me to think that Powick is just any old loony bin. They are very proud that the regime here has been opened up and modernised.

Powick Hospital opened in 1852 as the Worcester County Pauper and Lunatic Asylum. Its site was considered ideal because it was close to a main road for patient transport, but also the landscape gave a magnificent view towards the Malvern Hills. A ha-ha was used instead of a fence, in order not to interrupt this view.

The asylum was intended to cater for 200 inmates, but was later extended. Between 1852 and its eventual closure in 1989, a total of 36,000 people went there. In the old days it had various workshops, a gas works, a farm, brewhouse, bakehouse and a chapel.

During the 1950s the wards were gradually unlocked, and high walls around some areas were pulled down. This did not lead to any mass escape, and indeed very few patients wandered off. Eventually patients were positively encouraged to go out, firstly around the grounds, then to the local cafe and even into town.

Then in 1968 the hospital was shown in the TV programme World in Action. Some shocking scenes were filmed on one of the long stay female wards, where 78 elderly patients were living in cramped and unsavoury conditions.

The same year it was announced that the government was setting up, and funding, the Worcester Development Project (9). Powick Hospital was chosen as the pilot project for closing all mental hospitals in the UK and replacing them with general hospital psychiatric units, supported by a variety of community facilities. It was assumed that such a move will provide a more economical and better service, and data would be collected to assess that.

Many people at Powick suspected that Dr. Spencer had invited the making of the World in Action programme in order to achieve government support for this area.

10th September 1971.

The doctors are still trying to impress me about Powick Hospital, and I can see that they are actually very proud of the place. 'Did you know that Elgar was bandmaster here?' they said today. I thought they were joking, but apparently not!

The doctors at the Asylum in the 1870s showed an enlightened attitude by coming up with the idea of a series of orchestral concerts, as well as Friday night dances in the ballroom for the inmates. Edward Elgar, a young local violinist, played in the concerts, and in 1879 became Band Instructor. His job was to conduct the Asylum Band, made up of members of staff, for the Friday dances. The authorities paid him £30 per year, plus a few shillings for any compositions.

11th September 1971.

Keep away from the LSD Unit, the lunching doctors advised me today. What on earth is the LSD Unit, I thought. Apparently this is something else I didn't realise that Powick is famous for. At first I thought it meant that they treated LSD users or addicts, but in fact LSD is being used here as a treatment for mental illness. Is there no end to the surprises at Powick Hospital?

Pioneering work in the use of LSD for psychiatric purposes was developed here by Dr. Ronald Sandison (10), beginning in 1952. He called it psycholytic (mind-loosening) therapy, and applied it to severe depression and schizophrenia, amongst other things.

Dr. Sandison left Powick in 1964, and the therapy programme was continued by Dr. Spencer until 1972. About 680 patients were treated, with a total of over 13,000 administrations of the drug.

However, like many other kinds of treatment, it fell into disrepute, and the LSD Unit closed when Dr. Spencer retired. Years later, a group of these patients took out a legal claim for compensation, on the grounds that they still suffered flashbacks from the LSD experience. Most of the claims were rejected, but about 50 were settled out of court by the Health Authority in 2002.

21st September 1971.

I am still very much feeling my way. Eventually the psychiatrists will refer some patients, but at the moment they are not really clear how I could help. And neither am I, of course. It is going to be a matter of trial and error.

In the meantime, I am just hanging about and getting to know who is who. Fortunately hanging about is well catered for by the institution. I have discovered the Doctors' Mess, which is another room where they can retreat away from the madding crowd. After starting work at 9 am, there isn't long to wait until coffee is served in the Mess at 10.30. If you drink it slowly, this will last until noon, and then it is only half an hour until you can decently go to lunch. By the time you have eaten a hospital lunch, including pudding with custard, and sat down for a rest and gossip, it is 2 pm. Then you rush off to your office, but you could be back in the Doctors' Mess by 3.30 pm for afternoon tea. After that, there is just time to wind down before going home.

I don't think there is anyone who does actually spend the day like this, although a few of them are not far off it. My own excuse is that this is how to meet all the doctors and get to hear all the gossip about what actually goes on here. But sooner or later there will be real work to be done.

12th October 1971.

So far, I have been mainly giving tests to in-patients on the admission wards. I may be making a rod for my own back by being too helpful about this, but it seems the easiest route to take at the moment. Besides, I actually enjoy testing these people. You get answers and see behaviours that you don't get during an interview or a chat.

My testing routine, the style that I developed at the Maudsley and St. Augustine's, seems to be acceptable here. The psychiatrists seem to think that it is a technological improvement on what went before. They will carry on filling in referral forms saying *IQ please*, and I will give them clever-looking results covering verbal ability, visuospatial ability, verbal memory, visual memory, short-term and long term memory, and so on. I will occasionally detect significant discrepancies between these results which will signal the fact that the patient is impaired in some way, and this may tell us something about his clinical state or diagnosis.

If nothing else, I am giving the patients a bit of occupational therapy. I am allowed to take them away from the ward, walking along the corridors to my quiet office. After an hour of 'doing puzzles', we have a little chat, and then I see them safely back to their ward. At certain times of day the patients do have a break from the ward anyway, by going to the proper Occupational Therapy department, but they seem to regard that as merely a way of helping to pass the time. Whereas *seeing the psychologist* has an aura of importance.

Today I got an interesting result on my tests. A man admitted because of depression and slowness turned out to have all sorts of memory impairments and a weakness of his hand, which showed up only when doing a drawing test. Probably due to a stroke, rather than depression.

I enjoyed reporting these results to the consultant psychiatrist. Already I have noticed how pompous they get about their superiority to psychologists. Their view is that psychiatrists are expert not only in psychological problems, but also in physical medicine. Medically unqualified psychologists cannot be allowed to make clinical judgements, because they could quite easily miss serious physical problems, such as brain tumours. I have therefore now discovered a game which will make my work even more interesting: *Try to spot the physical diagnoses that these clever doctors have missed.*

6th December 1971.

I am beginning to get some therapy patients. The psychiatrists have gathered that psychologists can use behaviour therapy, but only to treat specific phobias. That might be the fault of the Maudsley, because recently they have been publishing lots of articles about their experimental work with specific phobias (such as spiders). The Maudsley people think that they can demonstrate scientific principles best if they start with simple problems.

So when one of the consultants saw an outpatient who was having anxiety attacks about getting on his motor bike, he referred him to me as a specific phobia. The man was certainly complaining specifically of his inability to face getting on his bike, which he had always loved riding.

Last week I started by showing him how to practise relaxation training and slow breathing, and today I was going to get him to start picturing himself getting on his bike (*imaginal desensitisation*). This could take many sessions, especially as I have never tackled this particular problem before.

But there was a miracle. When he arrived today he

swaggered in as a biker should. He reported that he was much better and was back on his bike, no problem.

The relaxation exercises had worked like magic, he explained. He had simply calmed down generally, and everything became easier, including the bike.

Further facts emerged which explained this. Apparently for some time there had been a situation at work which had been stressing him, until he started feeling shaky, which in turn made him feel unsafe on the bike. But now he had relaxed and overcome not only this nervousness but also the situation at work.

All in a week! I am amazed. It isn't supposed to be this easy. How am I going to explain this to the consultant who had set me the task of doing some proper behaviour therapy? I will have to say that he (and I, of course) had got the original diagnosis wrong. It was actually a general anxiety state, not a specific phobia.

We didn't do general anxiety states at the Maudsley, so I am going to have to work this one out for myself. Actually, it's quite simple if you use the idea that anxiety can make you anxious. Most people have some sort of worry about their anxiety symptoms (*Am I ill? Am I losing control? Am I weak? Will people think I am a fool?*).

Getting into a vicious circle of anxiety and worry is what had happened to the biker, but now that he has found a means of regaining control over himself (the relaxation techniques) he has stopped being afraid of his anxiety.

I was starting to develop as a Cognitive Behavioural Therapist, and thought I was moving beyond my Maudsley training. The term CBT was not yet in use, and even later on I was dubious about it. Behaviour Therapy was a much simpler term, and no one knew what Cognitive meant. Just more jargon to confuse the patient!

Behaviour therapy rests on the general principle of Behaviourism, which states that psychological matters can be studied scientifically by observing actual visible behaviour, without the need to discuss internal mental processes. It is based upon the principles of Classical Conditioning developed by Pavlov, and operant conditioning developed by Skinner.

Behaviour therapy emerged during the 1950s and 1960s. Then some elements of it started to combine with the cognitive (thought process) therapies of Beck and Ellis in the 1970s, leading to Cognitive Behavioural Therapy in the 1980s and 1990s. There is still a focus on the here and now and on symptom removal, using a combination of methods to modify both external behaviour and internal thoughts or feelings.

24th January 1972.

My magic cure by relaxation training is becoming popular. The psychiatrists are quite comfortable with this, as it seems like a form of hypnosis, with which they are familiar.

I watched one of the consultants doing his own style of hypnosis the other day, and was not impressed. There are some major similarities between hypnosis and relaxation training. The patient sits slumped, with eyes closed, while the clinician intones his sleep-inducing script. What troubled me was the condescending manner of the consultant towards his passive and grateful patient. None of that seemed very healthy to me. I must try not to get like that.

One problem with relaxation training is that it could become extremely tedious for me, if I am repeating it over and over again six times a day. But I have thought of a solution! I will acquire a tape recorder and make a recording of my very best soothing tones. Then I can simply play this to each patient, and they can do the relaxation exercise while I am thinking what to do next. Or even better, I could give them a copy of the tape to take home and practise every evening. In this way, they would get more practice, and it would feel more like self-help. On their visit to the clinic, they would get more time to talk to me. Or I could finish earlier!

31st January 1972.

I have acquired a tape recorder, with two speakers and a stereo microphone. This was my first purchase as a hospital employee, and it was unexpectedly easy. I just asked Dr. Spencer whether I could have one, and he sent me along to the electrical store in Malvern. 'Just get what you want, and tell them to send the bill to me'. The man in the shop seemed to know Dr. Spencer well, but inspected me carefully in case I was an escaped patient who was hoping to acquire a machine to blast the hospital with the sounds of Elgar.

This simple ordering system seems to have worked well, and the goods arrived this morning. I had no idea that it would then cause a huge fuss. Being rather pleased with myself, I mentioned my good fortune to the doctors at lunchtime. 'How did you get the money for it?', they asked. I explained how I had been sent to the shop by the medical superintendent, thinking that this was quite a funny story, bearing in mind the usual NHS bureaucracy and form-filling. But some of the doctors became quite angry, not with me, but with Dr. Spencer. 'When we ask him for anything, he says there is no money', they complained.

It seems that they have lots of grievances against Dr. Spencer. As medical superintendent, with his own house in the grounds and a laundry service provided by the patients, he has a long established position of power over everything that goes on in the hospital. Sometimes he rejects the requests of the doctors, and they suspect that he deliberately favours the likes of me in order to put them in their place. While they respect what he has done for the hospital in the past, they feel that he is now overdue for retirement.

I can't believe what a hornet's nest I have stirred up. Suddenly I have had a glimpse of medical politics. Fortunately, it seems that they are mainly fighting amongst themselves, and hopefully they will be too busy to turn on me.

21st February 1972.

I have now mastered the tape recorder. First I tried recording myself while seeing each patient, and then gave them this tape to take home, but these tapes sounded rather unprofessional. So now I have made a better quality standard tape to give to them all. The tape is only fifteen minutes long, but it took hours to make. I had to do it at home to avoid all the clattering noises you get in hospitals. I didn't dare ask for another recorder to make copies of the tape, so I have bought one for myself at home and will use this.

The relaxation tape has received the blessing of one of the consultants this morning. He announced that he had been trying it for his headaches. So it's all right, I can relax now. I am no longer the centre of scandal over having a tape recorder. Well, apart from the porters, who tease me with suggestions that I sit in my office all day listening to the hi-fi.

27th March 1972.

All this practice at making relaxation tapes has given me a habit of speaking very slowly and gently when seeing patients. This seems to make them think that I am a very nice and kind person, and some of them are extremely grateful for that. They tell me that I am the first person who has ever really listened to them. I am not sure whether to believe them. If it is true, it surely raises serious questions about all their friends and relatives.

I didn't know what to say this afternoon when a patient not only praised me for being easy to talk to, but then complained about the difficulty of talking to the psychiatrist who had referred him to me. 'He makes rude comments about how I look, and talks down to me. I feel really angry for the rest of the day, and can't get to sleep that night. And he asks whether I'm sleeping any better after taking his tablets!'

I tried to discuss this in terms of how the patient might deal more generally with anger generated by the confrontational attitudes of others, but really I felt that this was a significant complaint against the psychiatrist. This wasn't the first patient to have told me the same thing. I am beginning to wonder if my job might be easier if the patients did not have to see a psychiatrist first. One of the consultants seems to be telling these patients that they are only being referred to the psychologist because their problem is a minor one. The psychiatrists have to save themselves for really serious illness.

The patients are telling me all these things about the psychiatrists. Am I going to get as angry as the patients?

26th April 1972.

There was a political coup at the hospital today. I was sitting in the Doctors' Mess having coffee with some of the junior psychiatrists, when the three consultants arrived and announced that they had 'taken over'. Dr. Spencer was retiring, and the old-fashioned idea of having a medical superintendent in charge of the hospital was being abolished. Instead, there would be a group called the Executive Committee, consisting of the three consultants, the chief Nursing Officer and the Administrator. No single person would be in sole control. Decisions would evolve by negotiation and agreement.

The old regime was gone. The LSD unit was closed. Some people clapped their hands and said 'Good!', but others looked worried and wondered how this had been done without them knowing. Better the devil you know, they thought.

12th September 1972.

I have taken up smoking! This is a great surprise to me. I have always been a non-smoker, turned off by the choking clouds of smelly smoke produced by my father's pipe, and by my mother nagging at him about this. I had never even considered the possibility of trying it.

But in the hospital I was uncomfortably unique. Everyone smokes, absolutely everyone. Doctors, nurses and patients. There are ashtrays everywhere, beside every chair and on every desk and table. Standard Health Service glass ashtrays. Chrome ashtrays on stands in the corridors. Patients ask me for a light, and I keep a box of matches in my desk drawer in order to show my hospitality.

Then one of the psychiatrists asked me to set up a *token economy* in one of the long stay wards. This is a system in which patients showing good behaviour are given tokens, which they can save up to get real rewards. Some of these patients have gradually become mute over the years, possibly because they don't have any need to speak. The institution provides all their needs whether they ask for them or not. From now on these patients will be given tokens for any words (or even grunts) uttered. After collecting a few tokens, their prize will be a *cigarette*.

Giving them cigarettes would never have occurred to me, but the nurses insist that this is the only realistic option. *They will do anything for a cigarette.* So I went to the hospital shop and bought some. I didn't know what to ask for, but I remembered what a friend of mine smoked. 'Twenty Embassy, please', I said.

Next morning the nurses explained that I didn't need to personally supply the cigarettes for the token economy. The ward was supplied with cigarettes out of hospital funds, and each patient had his regular ration. They would simply give out some extra ones as rewards.

That left me with a packet of cigarettes in my desk drawer, and the idea that I ought to try one. I had always said that I could not understand why people smoked, and no one had ever explained it beyond saying that they enjoyed it. But why did they enjoy it? I'm a psychologist, for goodness sake! I ought to know these things.

So last night I sat down at home and tried to light a cigarette. After several false starts I got it going, and after several more false starts I was inhaling and coughing. After three cigarettes I was feeling sick and giddy, but also quite pleasantly interested.

Well, that will do, I thought. My curiosity was satisfied. No need to smoke any more.

But this morning I had my usual cornflakes and coffee for breakfast, and thought I would just try a cigarette to see if it had the same effect as it had last night. In fact, it was even better. I felt awake, confident, and ready to take on all the problems of the hospital. So I had another one on the way to work, and several more throughout the day. I bought another packet on the way home, just in case. I like being a smoker.

Although smoking has been frowned upon at various times for social or ethical reasons, it is only in recent years that it has been consistently viewed in a negative light. Medical studies have proved that it is a leading cause of various serious and fatal diseases. Although many people have succeeded in giving up smoking, many millions continue to do so, and young people all over the world still take it up.

When people start smoking, it provides pleasurable effects. There is a mixture of mental alerting and physical unwinding. But quite soon this becomes addictive, and the smoker is trapped in a cycle of withdrawal symptoms only relieved by having another cigarette. He may be unaware of this trap for many years.

30th September 1972.

Smoking comes in handy at parties. I hate parties. I am an introvert and proud of it.

There was a time, during my teens, when I thought that there must be something wrong with me. Normal lads were loud and they hung around with crowds of friends, while I enjoyed doing things quietly on my own. Attracting attention to myself made me nervous. Was that normal?

It was a great comfort, and a boost to my confidence, when I picked up that book by Eysenck on personality. He had collected a great deal of data on two dimensions or traits, Neuroticism and Extraversion, and had shown that they are quite independent of each other. This was just a mathematical fact, but it had great meaning for me. It meant that neither extraversion nor introversion have any bearing on whether you are neurotic. Extraverts might get more social admiration, but they have their own weaknesses and problems, and there is a lot to be said for being a quieter sort of person.

Parties are a bit of a nightmare for someone like me. Why

do all these people stand around shouting at each other because they cannot hear themselves speak over the sound of other people shouting at each other? I like to listen to people, and I can't hear a thing. So I stand there smiling and nodding and trying to look cool. This is easier with a drink in your hand, and even easier with several drinks in your stomach. But too many drinks and I start to fall asleep. So a cigarette does wonders. You can pose with a cigarette, and you don't have to drink too much. You can smoke one after another all night and still drive home.

If I don't go to the Powick doctors' parties, I will make myself an outcast. So I go, and smoke one after the other. There is alcohol as well, of course, as this is the main purpose of the party. Sparkling wine bought by the crate, paid for by the doctors' fees for signing death certificates.

There is a steady trickle of deaths on the long-stay wards of the hospital, which contain hundreds of rather elderly men and women. Almost all of them are cremated rather than buried, requiring an additional certificate from a second doctor. Each certificate earns the doctor a fee, and the doctors agreed to put all this money into a fund, which mounts up until it is enough to buy the required amount of wine.

Tonight's party has been a bit overdue, apparently. A real scandal. The hospital administrator who looked after the fund had unofficially borrowed it to cover a personal debt. This wasn't noticed until the doctor in charge of parties started wondering why it had been so long since the last occasion. The administrator has been sacked and reported to the police. It's a shame, he seemed a nice man. I was quite worried the other day when I saw him pacing up and down outside his office.

10th October 1972.

I had another magic cure today. It's very interesting when some patients get better very quickly for no obvious reason. They are extremely pleased, of course, but you don't know how it happened and therefore don't know how to repeat the trick.

You start off by doing a long interview with them, working out a plan of action for their anxiety and depression, which could take weeks or months of hard work to carry out. But then they come for their appointment the following week and report that they felt much better for just talking to you. Their life has returned to normal and there are no more problems left to tackle. How does that happen after they have had problems for months or years?

Today's case was even more bizarre, because it involved the *shock box*. This is a bit of equipment that I found in the department when I first came, and I had wondered whether it might have any use. It is simply a battery-powered device for generating a high voltage (but harmless) electric shock to the fingers of your hand, and is intended for use in Aversion Therapy. The patient thinks about, or actually carries out, his particular bad habit while at the clinic, and every time he does this, he is given a jolt from the shock box.

I have been reading an article about aversion therapy being tried out for the very difficult problem of stammering. People who have a severe stammer or stutter are usually quite distressed about their problem, and I must admit that it seems rather cruel to start giving them electric shocks. On the other hand, they can get very stuck with this problem, and maybe they would agree to almost anything that might help.

So, last week when I saw a man with a bad stammer, for which he had tried various treatments, I offered to try the aversion method. I explained that it would only be an experiment, with no guarantee of success. He would read something out loud to me, and if he got stuck on a stammer, I would press the button and give him a shock (a distraction from his more usual self-consciousness, perhaps?). But first I would just give him a shock to show him what he was agreeing to. I pressed the button, and he duly jumped in surprise at this sensation in his fingers.

So then I gave him a book and he started reading out loud. My finger was poised over the button, and I don't know who was more nervous, him or me. But he read beautifully, with no hint of a stammer, and I wasn't sure whether to congratulate him or feel that it was a bit of an anticlimax. He finished the reading and then carried on speaking perfectly. My instinct was to quit while the going was good, so I just gave him another appointment and said we would do the proper treatment next time.

But when he arrived today he reported that he had not stammered again. This kind of success is quite bewildering! All I could do today was to tell him to come back for more if he relapsed. Perhaps I should insist on people reporting back, because you never really know what happens to them. But you can't really hang on to patients just out of curiosity, can you?

17th October 1972.

Another shock box case. One of the consultants seems keen to get me to do aversion therapy, but I am very dubious about it. I think I will give it up after this particular case (has my aversion therapy cured me of doing aversion therapy?).

It has sort of worked, but not really. It was a married man wishing he could get rid of his homosexual urges. He is bisexual, sometimes more one way and then more the other. Although homosexuality was legalised in 1967, it is still illegal to visit public toilets for this purpose, and indeed the police make regular swoops on known haunts. There is embarrassing publicity for anyone caught in this way. My patient explained that he has a habit of going out at night to visit such toilets (going 'cottaging'). His wife suspects nothing, thinking that he is simply going out to the pub for a drink. He fears that he will be caught and then his wife will find out.

I have explained that I do not believe that I can remove his homosexuality, and indeed he says he cannot imagine being any different. But maybe he could change his risky habit of going around public toilets, and replace it with a more legal way of meeting people.

I have given him several sessions of looking at a random series of photos of men and women. When a male photo comes up, he looks at it and imagines meeting this person in a public toilet, at which point I give him a fairly hefty electric shock. When a female photo comes up, he is relieved to get no shock.

Until now this has seemed to have no effect, but today he sat down and said that there had been an unexpected result. He had been going into some toilets in the middle of Cheltenham, 'just for a pee', and suddenly he had felt his heart racing and he began to shake. It was like a panic attack, and he only managed to go in to the toilets because he was desperate for a pee. Otherwise he would have fled, he reckoned.

I'm not happy about this. Most of the time I am trying to help people with their phobias and panic attacks, not trying to create new ones. Hopefully his anxiety has not developed too far, and he can use it positively to remind himself not to go into toilets except when necessary. But I am going to extract myself from this case, and I am getting rid of the shock box.

Aversion therapies can take many forms. For example putting unpleasant-tasting substances on the finger nails to discourage nail-biting, using drugs to cause vomiting when someone drinks alcohol, or giving electric shocks for all sorts of problem behaviours. After some reports of success in changing homosexual behaviour in the 1960s, there was a burst of enthusiasm for this. Homosexuals volunteered for this treatment in preference to jail. Any form of homosexuality was illegal in the UK until 1967.

But eventually it was realised that the early studies were flawed. Any results that did occur were only in bisexuals, and not in people with a fully homosexual inclination. Society gradually came to terms with the fact that any particular sexual orientation is normal for that particular person. Aversion therapy for this purpose largely died out in the 1970's. People concerned about their sexuality are now offered counselling to come to terms with it.

25th October 1972.

I much prefer being nice to patients, reassuring them that nothing bad is going to happen, or coaxing them to do things they are nervous about. I am doing good business with agoraphobics and generally nervous people. These are all out-patients. I am not sure what they think about being sent out of town to the old mental hospital to see me here.

I am still keeping in touch with the hospital wards by doing tests on referred patients. However, the consultants have discovered another use for my tests, namely testing children in connection with decisions about their schooling. This is personally important to the consultants, who all have children of their own requiring the best middle-class education. This usually involves paying for them to go to a private school, if they are bright enough to be 'worth it'. In fact, according to my

IQ tests, their children are all well above average, as you would expect from genetic and family considerations.

As a working class lad who passed the eleven-plus exam to go to grammar school for free, I look at all this with a rather sceptical eye. The doctors' children are bright enough to do well in a state school, so why do they need their fathers to work long hours seeing private patients in order to fund their school fees? It's just a class thing, isn't it?

31st October 1972.

After testing their own children, I have been referred some others from the consultants' private practices. The consultants are Adult Psychiatrists really, but there is a shortage of Child Psychiatrists in private practice, so the occasional child gets seen.

When the child's IQ is not as good as the parent expected, it can be a bit like telling someone they have got cancer. Fortunately, most of my child cases have been very easy and rather pleasing. There was a girl of fourteen this afternoon whose mother had been upset by a bad school report. This was an expensive private school who had assessed the girl's exam prospects as only average. They had even done an IQ test which showed that she was just average. The girl's mother did not believe this, and wanted a second opinion.

She was right, in fact, as mothers often are. My tests showed the girl to be of high intelligence, but somewhat weaker in verbal attainment, and surprisingly even lower on a reading test. For some unknown reason, she had failed to learn to read as efficiently as she should have done. When the school tested her, they used a paper and pencil test, in other words a standard form to read and fill in. The results would have been affected by any difficulty in reading, so she scored misleadingly as only average. Whereas the test I used (the Wechsler Intelligence Scale for Children) is individually administered and includes many items which do not require any reading ability. It is a much more accurate measure of raw intelligence.

The headmaster of the school telephoned me the following week to express his disbelief at these results. He did not want to believe that the IQ test they had been using for years could sometimes be so misleading. He did not want to believe that his teachers could fail to spot a basic educational problem such as inadequate reading.

And he did not see how his school could cater for such a problem pupil. His school was for children without educational problems.

Unfortunately, I never heard what happened to this girl.

2nd November 1972.

The psychoanalyst climbed in through the window of the dining room today while we were having lunch. There is a long-established job here, with the title of Lay Analyst, meaning a trained psychoanalyst who isn't a doctor. There was originally an actual Jungian analyst (how many of those do you find in rural Worcestershire?), but now there is this young man who is a clinical psychologist just like me, except that he describes himself as a Psychotherapist. He is thrilled with his office, which has historical psychoanalytic features such as a couch and a soundproofed double door. This has enabled him to develop his interest in Primal Scream Therapy without frightening anyone passing in the corridor.

He is clearly an unconventional sort of person, and probably the only person in the hospital who would have climbed in through a window. It was quite understandable, of course. He was coming from a part of the hospital which is a long walk if you go round all the corridors, but which is only a short distance from the back of the dining room. The windows were wide open to let out all the cigarette smoke from the doctors and myself, and he is tall enough to reach the sill and haul himself in, so why not!

People sometimes ask me if patients ever escape from Powick Hospital. I can now say no, this doesn't happen, but passing psychoanalysts do sometimes climb in.

4

BLACK BOXES AND LIE DETECTORS

14th November 1972.

I am still looking for ways of applying science to the problems of mental illness. Biofeedback devices are very fashionable at the moment, and we have acquired some out of research funds. They all involve the patient being wired up to a box which detects their skin conductance (sweating), or brain alpha waves (non-alertness), or skin temperature, or muscle tension. The box gives out a buzzing signal when the patient's measurements are heading in the 'stressed' direction, and goes silent when the patient relaxes.

Supposedly this helps the patient to learn how to get themselves relaxed. But I am not sure that they really do any better than when they just relax without all these technical complications. I don't think I can be bothered with biofeedback.

Until research in the 1960s, it was believed that physiological processes (e.g. heart rate) were solely under the control of the autonomic nervous system and not responsive to conscious mental effort. Unfortunately, some of the early research which showed otherwise was later found to be flawed, and the results exaggerated. Other early efforts looked at the claims of mind/body control by yogis and others who meditate.

Interest in biofeedback has waxed and waned since the 1960s. It is undergoing a renaissance during the early 21st century, related to a general rise in interest in alternative medicine. However, definitive research is still lacking. Many people believe that the use of biofeedback equipment is an unnecessary expense, and can be replaced with simple relaxation training, meditation and self-hypnosis.

17th November 1972.

The trouble with these biofeedback boxes is that they don't give a proper measurement. They just detect changes and make buzzing sounds, so you don't know where you are, really. Perhaps we ought to stick with real scientific equipment, like the psychophysiological recorder (polygraph) that I inherited from the previous psychologist. This measures heart activity, skin conductance or breathing patterns, and draws them on a paper chart that rolls out of the machine for your inspection.

This does prove useful occasionally, like this afternoon when I was seeing a young man who is a terrible hypochondriac. He launches into long and involved descriptions of sensations in his chest, namely aches and pains and missed heart beats. A few years ago he saw his father die of a heart attack, and now he visualises the same thing happening to himself. Instead of trying to do something about the job stress that is the actual cause of his symptoms, he is totally preoccupied with his heart and whether or not it is functioning. He keeps telling us all about it, but we don't seem to understand, which makes him even more anxious and angry.

So I wired him up to the heart monitor section of the machine and recorded his ECG activity while he was describing what he was feeling. 'It keeps stopping and starting again', he insisted. Fortunately the chart was showing a perfectly sound and regular heart beat, nothing abnormal at all (later I got a second opinion from a doctor familiar with ECGs and heart problems). The patient looked at the chart coming out of the machine, and could see for himself that it was all quite regular. He became quite speechless for a while, giving me the chance to explain that his stress sensations had nothing to do with dying of a heart attack.

Unfortunately, when he came for his appointment today, he demanded another ECG recording to reassure him again. So OK, I did it all over again. I can see that this might just become another hypochondriacal habit, so I will have to move on to other strategies.

22nd November 1972.

If you want to wire a patient up to something, if only to give the appearance of being scientific, the simplest thing is a skin conductance meter. This measures the galvanic skin response of the body, which relates to sweat gland activity, which is obviously affected by stress and anxiety (as well as physical factors). The patient has an electrode on a finger of each hand, and a meter (with needle pointer) shows the amount of current flowing. As he relaxes, the reading goes down. But there are enormous differences between patients in their measurements, for no clear reason. I don't know what to make of it.

I was helping one of the doctors with a drug trial today, trying to see if a new tranquillizer is any more effective than the old ones. One of the measures being used is the skin conductance, which should reduce as the drug takes effect. The question is, by how much? One of the patients decided to tease me by asking whether there was anything unusual about his readings. I had to admit that they seemed very low for someone being treated for anxiety. He then confessed that he had been treated for excessive sweating by means of a sympathectomy. This is a surgical procedure for disconnecting certain nerves which govern sweating, and clearly it had worked in this man. Nonetheless, his skin conductance measures were behaving normally, going down as he relaxed. It was just his baseline level that was unusual.

The Church of Scientology has produced a type of skin conductance meter which they call an E-meter. Sessions are conducted by Scientology staff known as Auditors. The subject holds a pair of electrodes resembling cans, while the auditor asks a series of questions and notes both the verbal response and any corresponding electrical response.

According to the Church of Scientology, the E-meter is a pastoral counselling device that helps to locate spiritual distress or travail. It is also used in recruitment, when Scientologists offer stress tests to passers-by. It has been the subject of much controversy, for example in 1963 when the US authorities seized a hundred E-meters, accusing the Church of making false claims for the success of the meters in treating physical and mental illness. The Church was ordered to display a disclaimer on each machine.

The story of the E-meter is a good example of how a huge amount of controversy and hot air can be created from something that is nothing more than a very elementary technical device.

8th December 1972.

I'm off to America next week, in search of a new black box! One of the consultants spotted an advert for a 'new lie detector measuring anxiety in the human voice'. Like most psychologists, I am sceptical about lie detection, but if this equipment detects anxiety in the voice then it might be worth looking at for clinical purposes. The advert says that the person's voice is tape recorded and then electronically analysed by the machine, so there is no question of any wires being attached to anyone. That sounds neat, and it would be kinder to patients than wiring them up.

The advert suggested writing to the American manufacturers for more information, and somehow this has led to them giving me a free trip to their lie detector course in Washington. Presumably no one else in the UK has shown any interest, and they want to try to sell their first machine over here. That would be quite difficult for them, as we British do not believe in lie detectors as the Americans do.

The Dektor Corporation (originally called Dektor Counterintelligence and Security Inc.) was formed in 1969 by three former U.S. Army intelligence officers, Allan Bell, Charles McQuiston and Wilson Ford. They had expertise in polygraph lie detection and in electronics, and wished to produce a better type of lie detector. By analysing the voice, the whole process would be recorded for analysis (together with any confessions), and there might even be occasions when it could be done covertly (e.g. over the phone).

They produced the PSE (Psychological Stress Evaluator) in 1970. The original version used a multi-speed reel-to-reel tape machine to record the interview, which was later fed into the PSE equipment (which was contained in a smart black carrying case). The operator played each of the subject's replies at slow speed into the PSE, which used a heat pen on a rolling paper strip to draw a voice chart. This showed the voice electronically in terms of its fundamental frequency activity, and the aim was to detect a microtremor in the voice. This was seen as a modulation of the basic voice activity, i.e. the chart would wobble up and down.

The theory is that this microtremor reflects the general

physiological tremor which occurs in all muscles of the body, and that this is suppressed when the muscles become tense. A stressed voice will therefore cease to show any modulation, and the PSE chart will show straight or square patterns.

Later versions of the PSE became more sophisticated and computerised, but the principles remained the same.

19th December 1972.

I'm back, after five days in Washington on the Dektor course with a bunch of private detectives and security men. I expect they wondered what I was up to.

The trip was great (by jumbo jet). People kept saying how big the plane was, with 360 passengers. But this was my first time on any sort of plane, so I didn't know any different. On the way out we flew over the ocean near Newfoundland where you could see the icebergs. An awesome sight.

All this new technology was very exciting. The first Boeing 747 jumbo jet arrived at Heathrow airport from New York in January 1970. Within a year nearly a hundred jumbo jets were being operated, and seven million passengers had been carried. This plane has dominated the airline world for over thirty years.

20th December 1972.

Now I am trying to remember what I learned on the course. Also I need to decide whether the PSE is worth pursuing. At least I have decided that I will allow myself to call it a machine. The Dektor training staff had a game going with a swear box for anyone who used the word *machine*. They wanted us to say *equipment* for some reason, but I prefer *machine.* And that's what everyone else seems to call it.

I have no idea whether the PSE works. The private investigators on the course asked me what I thought. They thought I must be an expert on this kind of thing. Could it be just a hoax, they wondered? Even one of the trainers admitted that he had found it useful mainly as a tool in a dramatic performance aimed at triggering confessions. But I don't even know whether it does detect anxiety or stress, quite apart from the lie detection issue. It's an intriguing machine, though, and it would be great fun finding out whether it can measure anything at all. I want one.

The trouble is, it costs over a thousand pounds, and I work for the National Health Service which doesn't normally buy such things. Having said that, Powick Hospital did buy that CCTV system and a polygraph for the previous psychologist, and they would have amounted to a similar sum of money. So why not ask? My adventures with the PSE has cost them nothing so far. I will have to emphasise that the PSE is a Voice Stress Analyser, not a Lie Detector, and that it would be at the leading edge of modern scientific psychological research. Leading edges are very fashionable at the moment.

16th April 1973.

After a long story involving a consultant psychiatrist, the regional health authority research fund and Her Majesty's Customs and Excise, the PSE equipment arrived in Britain and was delivered to me.

Even if the PSE itself does not work, at least its Uher reel-to-reel tape recorder is of very high quality and will enable me to make better relaxation tapes. That should lessen my guilt at spending all this money on a black box. Mind you, it's a very smart black box, a strong and heavy Samsonite case which looks as if it might contain a large quantity of banknotes. And when you open it up, you see a solidly made machine with control buttons and a chart recorder, with the heat pen which will allegedly draw your innermost feelings on that roll of paper. I can see how impressed a suspect might be, if he believed in this lie detection stuff. There is even a brochure headed Dektor CIS, which sounds a bit like the CIA (referred to by one of the Dektor colonels as *Uncle Sam's Unmentionables*). I will have to hide this from my patients.

10th September 1973.

I have been playing with my new toy quite a bit, even taking it home to analyse tapes in the evenings, as there isn't enough time in the day. Quite a few small experiments have given reasonably positive results, so I am encouraged to think that there might be something in it.

For example, when people slowly count numbers out loud while they settle down in a chair and become relaxed, their PSE charts do show a corresponding decline in voice stress. I did of course get someone to shuffle the charts so that I wouldn't know which was which, otherwise I might have unconsciously cheated. You have to get the experimental design right.

Also I have found that the PSE stress patterns do increase when people talk about things that disturb them, although this is by no means a clear or simple effect. And I was pleased to find that people can, albeit with difficulty, hear and identify this stress in someone else's voice. For me, this makes it more real, not just some covert measurement on a chart.

I have sent my results to Dektor, in the hope that they might know if anyone else is doing this kind of research.

27th November 1973.

I have given in to temptation! When listening to politicians talking on the radio or TV, it is very easy to record them and then play this through the PSE. Are politicians like Ted Heath or Harold Wilson too smooth and practised to show stress when being evasive? Well, maybe. But they do show stress at certain times and on certain unexpected subjects, but not for any reason that I can interpret. Perhaps someone who knows more about current politics and politicians could find some meaning in it.

I don't think I can pursue this line of research, although I have heard that some people in the USA are using the PSE to try to analyse politicians' speeches, especially after the Watergate scandal.

14th May 1974.

Oh dear, I think Dektor are getting impatient to sell some machines in the UK. Apparently a security firm here has acquired one in connection with the vetting of candidates for jobs, and New Scientist magazine is starting a bit of a campaign against this. There are some examples of dubious practices in the USA, and we wouldn't want such things here. Not that I can imagine lie detection being taken seriously anywhere other than the USA.

The press have scented a story, and they seem to have been given my number.

The local Worcester newspaper this week had the headline

Hospital hopes to heal with lie detector. The journalist was impressed with what he called my *£2,000 James Bond-type super gadget.* He did write that I was hoping to use it to analyse and treat clinical anxiety problems. But he couldn't help noting that this was *a long way from the original purpose of the PSE - the high security, counter-intelligence world of Beretta automatics, dry Martinis (shaken not stirred) and mouth-watering bikini-clad girls emerging from a tropical sea.*

I did have an exciting day today, though. The machine and I appeared on Pebble Mill at One, from the BBC in Birmingham. I wore my best suit (actually my only suit), and somehow I managed to demonstrate how the PSE was operated, after which the studio audience dutifully clapped. I can't remember what I said, but probably something about detecting people's phobias.

15th May 1974.

A woman rang me today and asked if the PSE would help to treat her agoraphobia. I tried to persuade her to see her doctor, thinking that she could be referred to see me, but it turned out that she was in Kent. I hadn't realised that Pebble Mill at One was shown nationally, and not just in the Midlands. Oh dear, I wonder what I've started.

15th August 1974.

The hospital switchboard is beginning to complain about journalists ringing up and trying to find me. Indeed, I am beginning to get tired of repeating myself. I never realised that each journalist has to ask the same questions in order to call the story his own, nor how many journalists there might be in the world.

Today I was visited by a man from the Daily Mail who was keen to do a story about lie detection. The fact that the PSE test could be done over the phone gave him a new angle that had not been used by other journalists. Back he went to his office in London, and then he rang me and we went through a mock lie detection test concerning what age he might be. I was amazed to find that the machine got the right answer. At least it did so after I realised that I had messed up my logical interpretation of the scores.

This was probably just a fluke, although I have noted that this is not the first time that the machine seemed to work better over the phone than with face-to-face high quality recordings. Perhaps the poorer phone sound has had some unnecessary frequencies usefully filtered out of it.

14th March 1975.

Today I recorded the Lesley Whittle tape from the radio news, and played it through the PSE. It seems an almost indecent thing to do, so I haven't told anyone, but I thought I might be able to see some very highly stressed voice charts. My usual research subjects and patients are never hugely stressed, because I am seeing them in a relaxed environment. Whereas this poor girl who was kidnapped must have been at her wits' end when she made that phone call to her family.

The PSE charts did indeed show some extreme examples of stressed voice patterns.

On the night of 14th January 1975, Donald Neilson (who called himself the Black Panther, having committed robbery and murder at a series of Post Offices in the North and Midlands) abducted Lesley Whittle from her family's Shropshire home. He left ransom instructions, and later there was a call made by Lesley. The family attempted to cooperate with the kidnapper's demands, but got nowhere. On 7th March Lesley's body was found in an old mine shaft in Bath Pool valley, Kidsgrove.

24th March 1975.

There are plenty of other things going on in my life, such as new colleagues, students, lots of patients, and so on. But the PSE is always on my mind. Probably too much, but I feel the need to solve the puzzle and publish some decent research. This isn't just the usual attempt to gain professional status by generating publications. There is also the need to justify my expensive purchase of the PSE from Health Authority funds.

I am bothered by the way that Voice Stress Analysis has become inextricably linked with lie detection. Rational scientists everywhere think that lie detection is dangerous rubbish or pseudo-science, and therefore Voice Stress Analysis is tarred with the same brush. Maybe even as a measure of stress it will still prove to be rubbish, but we don't know that until we have done the research. Am I the only person working on this?

I have written to the New Scientist magazine, in response to their campaign against lie detectors. *Don't throw the baby out with the bath water*, I said.

28th August 1975.

New Scientist has persuaded me to write an article about the

PSE, and it was published today (11). It is very pleasing, obviously, getting something published in this well-known magazine. But of course they didn't let me get away from their agenda. *Secret lie detector in the lab* was the title they gave it.

And now they have persuaded me to join them on the New Scientist stand at the annual conference of the British Association for the Advancement of Science in Guildford. My job will be to demonstrate the PSE as a lie detector to any passing scientist willing to play the game. Oh, well, it's all a bit of fun and experience, I suppose.

4th September 1975.

Guildford was hard work. Going around carrying an unusually large case full of wiring makes you a bit self-conscious, especially in a place where the IRA had planted bombs the year before and a trial was in the news. When I went out of the hotel in the evening and left the PSE in the safe-keeping of the receptionist, I felt obliged to open it up and explain that it wasn't a bomb.

Then, on the first day of my three day stint in the entrance hall of the university, someone came up and asked if I was a Scientologist. The New Scientist people leapt to my defence at such a suggestion. Then we had a good laugh because I said I could have brought my skin conductance meter as well.

Anyway, I was kept surprisingly busy 'lie-detecting' volunteers about any small sins they might have committed, and managed not to make too great a fool of myself. I didn't make any false accusations, and there was the occasional success in detecting something. Just enough to keep the lie-detector myth going.

All sorts of people stopped at the New Scientist stand.

There was Magnus Pyke, of course, a famous figure from the television (and Secretary of the British Association for the Advancement of Science). He kindly posed for a photograph with me. And finally, when I was becoming too exhausted to speak, a man from the BBC World Service radio wanted an interview to broadcast to Australia. Strangely enough his tape recorder was the same model as mine.

The Guildford pub bombings occurred on 5th October 1974. The Provisional IRA planted bombs in two pubs that were popular with Army personnel. Five people were killed and 65 were seriously injured. The bombings were at the height of the Troubles in Northern Ireland. Three men and a woman were arrested, and in October 1975 they were sent to prison. After serving fifteen years, the appeal courts overturned the verdicts. The convictions had relied upon confessions which were obtained by torture, while evidence clearing them had been withheld.

9th December 1975.

The newspapers haven't finished with me yet. The Sunday Times wants me to try out some lie detection with the George Davis case. This is a man from the East End of London who was convicted in March of an armed robbery at the Ilford branch of the London Electricity Board in April last year. There has been a big campaign running to try to clear his name, including writing GEORGE DAVIS IS INNOCENT OK on railway bridges, and then sabotaging the Test cricket pitch at Headingley, Leeds. The campaign people are arguing that traditional East End criminals are normally content to do their time in prison if they did the crime, but in this case George Davis has been 'fitted up'.

George Davis himself is not available for a lie detector test, of course, as he is in prison. But the people who gave him an alibi are available and willing. So I have agreed to do it! My excuse is that this is a great opportunity to find out how it all works in a real live case. It seems unlikely that I will come up with the devastating conclusion that George Davis is guilty. Having read the arguments about the evidence, there seems considerable doubt about the verdict. I can always say that a lie detector test, however dubious, is no more ridiculous than the eyewitness identification problems that occurred in this case.

Some people have suggested that it is no bad thing for George Davis to be locked up, even if he didn't do this robbery. He is known to have criminal connections, and it is only a matter of time before he gets involved in something. But this is not how the law is supposed to operate. That kind of rough justice always leads to sloppy or corrupt police work, and that is no good for any of us.

The robbery for which George Davis was convicted ended up with a long chase, numerous vehicles being commandeered and several of the robbers getting injured. Unusually, the payroll attack was observed and photographed from the beginning by undercover police officers. In addition, members of the public gave statements. Unfortunately there were many inconsistencies in the witness statements and photographic evidence. A number of blood samples were recovered, but did not match with George Davis. This evidence was not made available to the court.

The reliability of eyewitness identification has attracted concern from the legal profession in England for at least a hundred years. Witnesses tend to be overconfident about their ability to pick out the right person, even when they are totally wrong. Observation and memory are easily distorted, especially in stressful situations.

After each series of miscarriages of justice, there tends to be a renewed focus on this issue. For example in 1969 a man was convicted of a crime after being identified by eight witnesses, despite having an alibi. The real perpetrator was discovered later. This and other cases led to the Devlin report in 1976, which established a requirement that in cases of disputed identification the trial judge must caution the jury about the dangers of eyewitness identification evidence. The judge should point out that confident eyewitnesses may be mistaken, and should instruct the jury to consider carefully the circumstances of the identification.

10th December 1975.

I'm going to look back on this some day and think how weird it was to have this bunch of East End characters in my office at Powick Hospital in the Worcestershire countryside. They arrived this morning after driving up from London, and it took me several hours to explain things and do the tests. There were the men who were originally charged along with George Davis (but who were found not guilty). And there were non-criminal witnesses who knew George Davis and who had given him alibis for the time of the robbery.

I had set up a list of standard questions for them all, concerning whether they had seen George Davis at the time of the robbery, whether they thought he had done it, whether they themselves had anything to do with it, and whether they knew anyone who had. These questions were interspersed with various neutral ones, and the whole list was asked twice to check reliability.

Although some of these people scored generally higher stress than others, there was no pattern of specific stress on specific questions. The least stressed people were the noncriminals who were giving George Davis an alibi. So I was quite happy to say that there was no evidence of lies being told.

14th December 1975.

It's all in the Sunday Times today! The headline is *Lie detector okays George Davis alibi.* But his appeal was turned down on the 11th December, so I don't know where they go from here.

18th December 1975.

I have had a ticking off from the health authority about appearing in the press and associating the name of Powick Hospital with these criminal matters. However, no one at the hospital seems too bothered. Indeed one of the consultants reckoned it was a good thing because *patients would be more likely to tell us the truth if they are frightened of being lie-detected.* He actually seems quite serious about that!

However, I think I had better not do any more of this kind of thing, at least not publicly. Not that I want to. The George Davis case was a one-off, just for the experience, and because I felt that it could do no harm.

8th April 1976.

Somehow I was persuaded to make a speech in the Houses of Parliament (in one of the committee rooms). I'm not really sure how it came about, but it was chaired by Alan Beith of the Liberals. My job was to give a ten minute talk on my lie detector results for the George Davis case. All the East End people were sitting there very politely, plus various other people that I didn't know. My eye was then caught by the sight of Michael Heseltine sitting at the back, smoothing his hair occasionally. This made it feel a rather important occasion, and I gathered that the idea was to try to persuade the Home Office to do something about the George Davis case.

After all the hysteria that has surrounded the case so far, I thought it best to be as coldly rational as possible. First I made a personal statement. *I hold no brief for George Davis. As far as I know he might have carried out all the robberies in London for the past twenty years.* I could see some of the East End people looking a bit shocked at what I might be going to say. *But the question is whether he did this particular robbery.* The East End people nodded firmly with relief. *I also hold no brief for lie detection. The reliability is nowhere as good as advertised. But in this case there were several people whose results could be cross-checked against each other, and I thought this might give better reliability.* I'm not sure if this is true, but it sounded good. *Even if the reliability of lie detection is poor, it might be no worse than the accuracy of eyewitness identification evidence as relied upon in this case,* I argued.

Finally I pointed out an issue that was being overlooked in all the fuss about whether George Davis and some of these other men were criminals and liars. There were at least two nice law-abiding people who had given George Davis an alibi, and the verdict of the court was making them out to be liars. Was this fair on them?

Alan Beith thanked me, and I came home somewhat amazed at my performance. Public speaking is not my best talent, and normally I stick to a script, but this seemed to flow quite easily.

In May 1976 the Home Secretary, Roy Jenkins, on completion of a police review of the case, agreed to recommend the release of Davis (by exercise of the Royal Prerogative of Mercy) because of doubts over the police evidence. This was a highly exceptional decision. Although the conviction was deemed to be unsafe, Davis was not declared innocent.

Then in September 1977, George Davis was caught red-handed at an armed robbery at the Bank of Cyprus, and was jailed again until 1984. Everyone who had campaigned on his behalf felt completely let down, especially his wife Rose, who rapidly got a divorce. She tells the story in her autobiography, completed shortly before her death from cancer (12).

George Davis continues to seek further reviews of the evidence in the Ilford case, hoping to finally establish his innocence of that particular crime.

14th May 1976.

I've been getting a lot of phone calls and letters from people wanting to have lie detector tests, mostly to prove their own innocence, but occasionally to prove the guilt of others.

Some of them are famous cases, which I definitely can't touch because there would be publicity, and my employer would be upset. It's all nonsense, anyway. Lie detector tests wouldn't do any of these people any good. Peter Hain, the anti-apartheid campaigner, is a good example. He was arrested for supposedly robbing a bank, on the basis of dubious eyewitness identifications, and despite having an alibi. When his solicitor rang me, I suggested that it would be better to concentrate on the eyewitness statements rather than introduce the distraction of lie detection, which in any case would not be admissible as evidence.

Peter Hain came to the UK from South Africa as a teenager in 1966. He became a leading figure in the anti-apartheid movement, and in 1973 he was convicted of criminal conspiracy in connection with the Stop the Tour campaign (which disrupted matches involving the South African rugby and cricket teams).

In 1976 he was cleared of the bank robbery, and there were allegations of conspiracy by the South African security services to frame him, but others think that it was just ordinary mistaken identity.

Then there was the case of John Stonehouse. His solicitor rang me and asked if I could help, but I couldn't see how lie detection could be applied even if you believed that it worked. It seemed that Mr. Stonehouse was more or less willing to admit that he had behaved in various illegal ways, but he wished to demonstrate that his motivations were good and honest ones. I excused myself on the grounds that this is technically not feasible.

John Stonehouse was a British politician and minister under Harold Wilson. He is perhaps most famous for his unsuccessful attempt at faking his own death in 1974. He had set up a number of companies, and by 1974 most of them were in financial trouble. He had been cooking the books, but then became aware that he was being investigated. After setting up a new identity, he fled after leaving a pile of clothes on a Miami beach (comparisons have been made with the BBC comedy series The Fall and Rise of Reginald Perrin).

He was presumed dead, and obituaries were published. In reality, he was on his way to Australia, where he hoped to start a new life with his secretary Sheila Buckley. He was discovered by the Australian police, who initially mistook him for the other missing Englishman, Lord Lucan.

At the trial he conducted his own defence, but he was convicted of fraud and other offences, receiving a seven year prison sentence. He was given an early release in 1979 after three heart attacks, and in 1988 he died of a further heart attack.

21st June 1976.

You get an awful lot of letters if you have a lie detector. Strange letters about strange things, and very long letters which have very large holes in their stories. I feel I have to write extremely careful replies to these people. I try to offer them some wisdom, but I really cannot touch these cases, certainly not with the PSE.

From a Solicitor:

We have a client who has been charged with driving a motor vehicle when unfit through drink or drugs. The surprising thing is that our client was not driving the vehicle, nor has he ever driven a vehicle. When the accident took place, our client got excited and he told the police officer that he was driving because he was aggravated by the attitude of the driver of the other vehicle, as well as the other witnesses.

It is understood that you have a device or method which can prove whether a witness is speaking the truth or not. If so, we can then request that the prosecution should have their witnesses subjected to such a test.

From a Solicitor:

Practically every case we have involves lies on one side or another, and sometimes these lies involve police officers. One might almost say that in almost every case there are allegations that the police are fabricating evidence. As defenders of people we have constant problems with this sort of thing, and we would love to have available even the threat of lie testing.

From a Solicitor:

We act on behalf of a client who is charged with making threatening telephone calls. Our client denies the charges. The prosecution have a tape recording of the phone calls, and they allege that the voice is that of our client. Counsel have requested that a voice specialist be instructed so that tests can be carried out to ascertain whether it is our client's voice.

From a man in Lancashire:

Having seen your name and address in the Guardian, I should be grateful for any light you can throw on a psychological problem which puzzles me, namely the taboo on nakedness.

From a woman in Surrey:

Two years ago I had my name removed from the list of patients of a local GP for personal reasons, never dreaming of the repercussions which would ultimately follow. I have endured outrageous violation of my privacy, in that the GP in question has had me kept under constant surveillance, using other patients and her friends to observe my comings and goings from my house, which unfortunately is on a corner and can therefore be observed by all and sundry. Telephone calls (of this I am sure) have been passed to various points along any route that I might make during the course of shopping.

The matter has been reported to every source that I can think of who might do something about this harassment, including the police, who I regret to say took no action whatsoever. I was simply told that I was suffering from delusions and a persecution complex. This I feel makes me out to be a liar, and I am more than willing to be a guinea pig for your lie detector.

From a man in London, to his children:

Regrettably, for reasons I haven't yet fully understood, your Mum has always refused to join me in Marriage Guidance or *psychoanalytical sessions. These to my way of thinking are essentially truth-seeking operations. You girls may or may not know that one of the assertions made in my divorce petition reads, in typical legal language, that she has sought by dissimulation to gain tactical advantages over the Petitioner (I am what the lawyers call the Petitioner, by the way).*

The verb dissimulate is described in my dictionary as concealing or disguising the true nature of anything in order to deceive, dissemble, feign or counterfeit. The verb dissemble is in turn to conceal, to make anything seem other than it really is, to hide under a false exterior, to disguise or misrepresent one's real feelings or motives or plans.

If, as your Mum says most often (but not consistently), that any question of reconciliation is nonsense, then I am happy to sacrifice my financial interest in our (formerly happy) family home. My preconditions for such a settlement would include the following:

That your Mum fully cooperates with me, in the presence of you three girls (and our Solicitors, if Mum wishes) in an uncomplicated truth-seeking session with a psychologist who I have managed to trace. This very professional and totally impartial gentleman is in possession of the only Psychological Stress Evaluator in the country, which reveals where the truth is being repressed or distorted.

Mum, for example, may ask him to find out whether I was telling the truth when I denied adultery during my argument with her last year.

From Mum I think we would all be interested to know whether she was being quite honest when she denied opening and re-sealing my mail in April last year, and whether she actually (in spite of her subsequent denials) said to me, shortly before leaving for Australia, that she loved me more than I will ever know.

If this deal is rejected, I will sadly allow the divorce proceedings to go through the courts with as much acrimony as Mum might care to inject into them.

17th August 1976.

I have found some uses for the PSE machine which are much more straightforward than stress measurement. For example we were doing some research to see if you can measure how depressed a patient is by how slowly he speaks. Instead of trying to time the speech with a stop watch, it is much easier to play a recording of it through the PSE and measure the chart with a ruler. Unfortunately our results were unclear (13).

Then today there was a case with an unexpected result. A man had been admitted to one of the wards in a state of distress and agitation because he was getting paranoid about something he could hear on his television. He had actually made a tape recording of the BBC news, and said he could hear something, perhaps voices, in the background. Neither the consultant psychiatrist, nor any of his assistants, could hear anything. The psychiatrists then came up with the idea of getting me to put on a show of analysing the tape with all my electronic equipment, after which I would assure him that there was nothing there.

OK, that was worth a try, so I played his tape through the PSE, and lo and behold there really was something on it! It was just a regular bleep of some kind, so faint and short that our ears weren't detecting it, but the chart shows these spikes appearing every second or so. I have no idea what these are, really, but the patient lives near to the Droitwich BBC radio transmitter which is well known for causing breakthrough interference in that area. So maybe that is what he can hear, and then he is misinterpreting it.

7th February 1977.

I have had more results published (14), supporting the idea that the PSE does measure anxiety. This was a repetition of some earlier work, using more people and a better scoring system. For example, listeners calling a phone-in radio programme about their problems had greater voice stress than professional radio journalists, as you would expect. And patients suffering from agoraphobia or social phobia (who would be anxious about coming to see me) had more voice stress than patients who were not phobic in that way.

The trouble is, these results are just statistical differences between large groups of data (which takes me hours to process), and I am beginning to lose my grip on what it actually means. What exactly am I looking at in these voice charts?

I have looked at the construction of the PSE machine and worked out the probable circuit (a fairly simple one), and I have read everything I can find on the 'Lippold microtremor' which is the suggested origin of the modulations seen in the charts. But there are more questions than answers, and I am beginning to feel stuck. The other day another researcher asked me whether I would recommend using voice analysis in his area of work, and I realised that I could not do so. *It's very unclear. Now you see it and now you don't,* was how I rated it. That's not good enough.

I dare say I will continue to tinker with voice analysis, but other professional matters are beginning to take my attention. Sooner or later I am going to have to give it up. I haven't the time or resources to crack this problem.

Since the invention of the Dektor PSE, other types of voice lie detector have been produced by other companies. Some are digitalised versions of the PSE, and others are based upon entirely different principles.

Each type of lie detector has proponents who argue fiercely that the other types of lie detector are rubbish. Against all of the voice analysers there are still the polygraph operators, who say that they are the only true lie detectors.

And of course the scientific world says that lie detection is just plain rubbish anyway, and that its continuing popularity depends entirely on myth encouraged by charlatans. There is considerable scepticism about the Lippold microtremor theory as a basis for voice analysis.

There has been no further progress in establishing voice patterns as a measure of anxiety or stress or arousal. Thirty years on, my 1977 study is still being quoted by PSE operators in support of this machine, although of course anyone who reads it will see that it is irrelevant to lie detection.

5

THE NEW HOSPITAL

The Worcester Development Project began in 1968 when the Department of Health and Social Security brought together the Worcester and Kidderminster Hospital Management Committee and the County Council in a coordinated joint planning venture. Powick Hospital was chosen as the UK location for testing the hypothesis that closing an old mental hospital and replacing it with general hospital psychiatric units, supported by a variety of community facilities, would provide a more economical and better service.

As well as new psychiatric units at Worcester (Newtown) and Kidderminster, day facilities were opened in Malvern, Evesham, Droitwich, Kidderminster and Worcester. Research studies, which were part of the Project, suggested that in general it was serving local people well. The main failures were that the planning and building of the main facilities took much longer than expected, and therefore the final closure of Powick Hospital did not occur until 1989 (because there were still significant numbers of old long-stay patients left without alternative accommodation).

A major general conclusion was that the need for short-stay beds (and possibly for day facilities) had been overestimated. At the same time the need for beds for the elderly, and for homelike accommodation for people with chronic illnesses, had been underestimated (15).

18th December 1978.

We have moved out of the old Powick Hospital and into the brand new psychiatric unit on the outskirts of Worcester. This is officially called Worcester Royal Infirmary (Newtown Branch), in the hope of removing the stigma of the mental hospital by making it part of the general Worcester hospital group. Indeed the fields next to it are where the new Worcester district hospital will be built, if the money ever becomes available. However, some cynics are already saying that people will simply call it Newtown Hospital, and *going into Newtown* will develop the same pejorative meaning as *going into Powick.*

It's amazing, everything being brand new. We were warned by the manager that we would not be allowed to take our favourite old chairs. All the furniture is squeaky clean and of matching modern design. And actually very comfortable.

There's just one uncomfortable aspect of the building. Half of the offices are arranged around a central courtyard, so you look out of your window straight into the windows of the offices on the other side, which isn't far away. The only way to get any privacy is to draw your blinds and pretend that you are happy about sitting in a windowless box. Luckily for me, as Head of Department, I have managed to get myself one of the offices on the outer side of the building. I can see all the people coming up the stairs, and even a bit of sky.

But whatever the snags, it's like being back in civilisation again. I was so keen to get into the new hospital that I moved the department here a week before everyone else. Some of the psychiatrists have been grumbling about leaving Powick, and I can see what they mean. Powick did represent asylum, with peace, space and country views, whereas Newtown looks like a busy cramped office block. Also I suspect that the isolation of Powick allowed the psychiatrists to go about their business largely free of external scrutiny, whereas at Newtown they will be subjected to greater managerial interference.

That applies to the psychologists as well, of course, but I will welcome that. We have nothing to hide. It is time for change. I have gone on too long keeping the psychiatrists happy, letting them get away with unwarranted pronouncements about what we can or cannot do. My research with the voice analyser hasn't really got anywhere, so it is time for me to focus back on to the everyday business of helping patients. The Trethowan report has told psychologists that we need to get ourselves better organised in a wider variety of specialties. This is a rallying cry from national level which has somewhat ruffled the feathers of the local psychiatrists.

The Trethowan Report (16) was sponsored by the Department of Health and written by William H. Trethowan, Professor of Psychiatry at Birmingham University. In his introduction to the report (1977), Trethowan summed up the current situation as follows:

In former times the clinical psychologist's role consisted largely of undertaking routine psychological measurements such as intelligence testing at the request of psychiatrists and other doctors, and represented in effect an ancillary service to the medical profession. Recent years have seen a substantial expansion in the body of psychological knowledge, accompanied by the development of new techniques which have major implications for treatment. One of the effects of these developments has been to make psychological assessment a much more sophisticated process with a wider range of implications, both in determining various aspects of individual need and in evaluating the progress of patients and their response to different forms of therapy. At the same time psychologists have developed a number of new forms of treatment, some of which have been widely applied and represent an important addition to the range of therapeutic resources.

The report noted that there has been a significant increase in the numbers of clinical psychologists employed by the NHS. It recommended the setting up of organised Area-based psychology services, and a proper career structure. In 1974 the NHS had undergone a major reorganisation, with the birth of Areas and Districts in place of the old local management committees, and psychologists (and lots of others) did not know where they stood in all this.

The Trethowan Report stopped short of recommending professional independence for psychologists. Indeed it stated that medical responsibility should not be taken by psychologists, and all cases should be screened by a psychiatrist or other doctor before referral to a psychologist.

However, Trethowan drew attention to the fact that psychologists could specialise in different fields of work, namely Physical Handicap, Mental Handicap, Child Health (child psychiatry and paediatrics), Neurology, Mental Illness (including forensic psychiatry and psychotherapy), Geriatrics, Adolescent Services, and Primary Health Care. This meant that psychologists could be working with, and taking referrals from, a variety of types of doctor (not necessarily psychiatrists).

20th December 1978.

Two of the consultants have long since made it clear that they regard the Trethowan report as dangerous nonsense, and that they will not tolerate any psychologist who tries to deviate from the psychiatric party line. I am beginning to find them quite offensive in the way that they talk over coffee. Having been quite close to them all these years, taking them with a pinch of salt, I could just carry on working round them. But my younger colleagues see no reason to cosy up to the psychiatrists as I have done, and perhaps they are right. It is time to start detaching myself from these people.

The first obvious move is to stop the old routine of having coffee, tea and lunch with them. The new hospital is an opportunity to break from old traditions. Before it was even built, the manager was making the point that there would no longer be a separate dining room for doctors (and psychologists). All staff will eat in the splendid new canteen, thus promoting the new multidisciplinary attitude between the various professions. But it turns out that the doctors still have a coffee room of their own, and I have decided to withdraw from that. The psychology department will have its own kettle (despite the attempts by the manager to persuade us to put money in the privatised coffee machine at the bottom of the stairs). It is time for the psychologists to be psychologists.

Of course, these Worcester psychiatrists were not the only ones who wanted to stem the tide of the psychological revolution. There were similar attitudes in many parts of the country. However, I would guess that there were a lot of psychiatrists who had no problem with psychology, but these ones tended to remain silent in the face of their more dominant colleagues.

At one point a letter was published in the Psychiatric Bulletin (17), expressing the irritation that a consultant psychiatrist felt with expanding professions such as social workers and psychologists. It went as follows:

We have found particular difficulty in the last year or two in our relationship with our clinical psychology colleagues, and this would seem to be primarily the fault of the Trethowan report, or perhaps its over-enthusiastic application.

Clinical psychology, having at one time been a profession that worked within the psychiatric hospital and under the umbrella of consultant psychiatric cover, has now become a district-based service doing its own thing, which in practical terms seems to mean that it has set up as a rival therapeutic group practising its own brand of therapy, and in competition with the established NHS psychiatric service.

Indeed, a rival therapeutic team is now in our area giving sessional time at health centres, and direct referrals are being made for treatment by general practitioners to these non-medically qualified therapists, presumably with the general practitioner continuing to take the legal responsibility for the patient. In practice this is leading to a demarcation dispute where it would seem that the clinical psychologists now consider that they are the experts in the treatment of neuroses, and that the psychiatrists should confine themselves to psychotic illness and the dementias!

I cannot think that these trends are healthy to psychiatry as a profession, since our own caseloads are absurdly large in contrast to those currently accepted by the other professions (clinical psychology and social work), resulting in fact in our probably giving a poorer service, but being unable to expand our own professional team because of financial constraints.

It would seem to me that the implications of the Trethowan report were not really thought through at the time, and that the way in which the situation is developing is something which should be causing psychiatrists a considerable disquiet.

5th February 1979.

The consultant psychiatrists are keeping up a continual stream of comments indicating that the Trethowan report will never be put into action in the Worcester area. Trethowan might be the Professor of Psychiatry just up the road in Birmingham, and a nice sort of chap, but clearly he is out of touch with reality (that's what they say). Somehow he has been conned into writing these things. But never mind, our more realistic psychiatrists in Worcester will defend the honour of their profession by making it go away. All they need to do is just ignore it. Alan Smith won't be any trouble.

This is something I am going to have to think about very carefully. I know what these consultants are like. You can't query anything with them, they always know best.

If I challenge them about Trethowan, they will get nasty, and that would mean war. You should never fight battles you cannot win, so I need to manoeuvre myself into a position where there is a reasonable chance. I'm not there yet. In fact it is all very daunting, and it would be tempting to sit back and not rock the boat. But I can't do that either, as the clinical psychology profession nationally is pushing us all in the direction of Trethowan. I can't very well go against that tide. It is now official National Health Service policy, even if our psychiatrists think otherwise.

In the meantime I must try to get on with my work. I didn't come into clinical psychology to spend all day playing professional politics.

19th February 1979.

Dealing with your patients' problems is a lot easier than dealing with these consultants. And sometimes you get a good laugh, even when things have a serious side.

I've been having some bizarre adventures with Mrs. Rowe's bird phobia, for example. At first glance, a phobia of birds doesn't sound hugely serious, and indeed there are lots of worse problems, but actually it can be a significant hindrance to normal everyday life. If you can't walk through town because of all the pigeons that strut around in the main street, and even going into your back garden gives you a panic attack, this is no joke. The humour was in my attempts at therapy.

The first thing that happened was the pigeon on the windowsill. It was during Mrs. Rowe's first appointment with me, when I was explaining about desensitisation and how we would start with really easy things like pictures, before moving on to real birds (perhaps someone would lend me a cage bird?). I could see her cringing, and she asked whether I had arranged *that*, pointing to something behind me. Puzzled, I glanced round and saw a pigeon sitting on the sill outside the window, looking in. I thought it wise at this point to close my blinds and shut out the pigeon, which then flew off, of course.

But strangely I have begun to notice that this bird appears on my windowsill every time that Mrs. Rowe is due. It doesn't seem to come on other days. I must be imagining this, but I can see why some phobic people start feeling that they are being actively pursued by their demons.

After several sessions with Mrs. Rowe, talking about birds and teaching her to relax and breathe slowly, I was wondering how to start introducing her to real birds. Getting hold of your patient's phobic objects can be quite a problem (when you want to dig up a worm from your garden, for example, they all seem to disappear. And quite how you arrange for thunderstorms to erupt overhead, I really don't know. Tape recorded thunder is no good). I was chatting about this to my brother-in-law, who teaches poultry science at an agricultural college. He once brought home a box of newly hatched chicks, cute little balls of fluff, the sort of thing that might just melt a bird phobic's heart.

He revealed that the college has a kind of poultry museum, full of all the different breeds of chickens, once alive but now stuffed and on display. I wasn't sure that chickens were really the sort of bird that troubled Mrs. Rowe, but beggars can't be choosers, and I accepted his offer to lend me one. *Only a small one*, I said. I have had previous experience of asking people to find other things, like spiders, and they always come with the biggest and hairiest specimen that you have ever seen. They can't get away from the mistaken idea that bigger ones should do the most good. So what does my brother-in-law come home with? A huge Rhode Island Red rooster. A magnificent specimen mounted on a wooden stand. Mrs. Rowe would surely have a fit.

This afternoon I had it all planned out. I placed the rooster safely hidden away on the table in the conference room at the other end of the corridor, and trained our closed circuit TV camera on it. Mrs. Rowe arrived, and I explained that there was a rooster in the building, safely dead of course, but quite big. I held my hands apart to indicate something nearly two feet across. She looked very worried and didn't think she could be in the same room as such a creature, however dead.

I explained about the closed circuit TV link. Yes, she was willing to have a look at the bird on the TV screen in my office. She looked at it rather dubiously, but yes, that wasn't as bad as she had expected. So then I explained that she could come out into the corridor and peep through the little window in the conference room door, to see the bird itself twenty feet away on the table. Very nervously she approached the window, as if expecting to see something horrific on the other side. Eventually her mind accepted that the bird was not going to charge towards her, and she agreed to enter the room, keeping well away from it. Several more steps and half an hour later, she was standing next to the bird and gingerly touching its feathers.

After several more sessions with the rooster, as well as practising at home by going out into her garden to sit watching the birds, she made good progress with her phobia. Then, by sheer coincidence, another patient of mine was trying to dispose of his house contents because he was moving to Australia, and for some reason he mentioned that he had a stuffed woodpecker. Naturally, I begged this from him, and presented it to Mrs. Rowe as a parting gift when I discharged her. She could keep this on display at home and use it as a reminder to carry on with her therapy.

27th February 1979.

One of my outpatient therapy patients has a strong suspicion that Newtown must be just like the hospital in *One Flew Over the Cuckoo's Nest* (which has nothing to do with bird phobias, unfortunately). He watches a lot of films on TV and even reads the books they are based upon. He prides himself on being involved in contemporary culture, including the consumption of a certain amount of cannabis. However, his problem is severe agoraphobia, and I have always reassured him that there is no question of him ever needing to go into a mental hospital.

One Flew Over the Cuckoo's Nest is a 1975 American drama film based upon a 1962 novel by Ken Kesey. It is set in a state mental hospital in Oregon, in particular a ward run by Nurse Ratched. She is a calm but unyielding tyrant who controls the patients with a combination of subtle humiliation in group therapy, punishment disguised as unpleasant medical treatments (ECT and lobotomy), along with a mind-numbing daily routine. After various dramas between the characters, two patients end up dead, one escapes, and Nurse Ratched is half-throttled.

While these sorts of things have been known to happen

occasionally in mental hospitals, especially in the past, they are exaggerated in the film by being condensed into a couple of hours of drama. In real life you could go into a mental hospital and be lucky enough not to see anything of the kind.

Mr. Markham really has no need to go into hospital, because his main therapy involves trying to persuade him to leave the safety of his home and walk up the street, or travel by car to other places. Some day he might be persuaded to venture into a shop. If he tries to do any of these things he starts shaking and has difficulty breathing. I visit him at home every week and take him out somewhere to try to build up his confidence, but progress has been disappointingly slow. In fact he has been like this for several years, and has ended up unable to go to work.

Last week his wife was very worried about him, and he seemed unusually down and desperate. Normally he keeps a cheerful facade despite his problems. I couldn't persuade him to try our usual trip out. Suddenly I found myself asking *How about coming into hospital for just a few days?* It wasn't that he needed any medical attention, but going into hospital was another fear that maybe he should face. If he goes and sees that Newtown is nothing like a madhouse or Cuckoo's Nest, perhaps he can stop tormenting himself about how he might end up. *I will fetch you out of hospital whenever you want,* I promised him, to show that he wouldn't have to escape through a smashed window as happened in the movie.

The consultant agreed to give him a bed, the ward being half empty at the time, and Mr. Markham settled into Newtown somewhat tensely, but the nurses were kind and he confessed that he was pleasantly surprised. But then the winter snows came, more and more snow over several days, until the roads were becoming impassable. Mr. Markham began to get anxious about being trapped, unable to get home, so I lied and told him that the roads were not as bad as people were saying. That was yesterday, and I promised to bring him home today, thinking that the snow might have lessened by now. Unfortunately it was really bad this morning, so I thought I had better get him home before it got even worse. That drive was a bit of a nightmare, slipping and sliding on the hill, but we made it.

The following week he reported that the whole experience of going to and staying in the hospital had perked him up again. He was still agoraphobic, but at least he was ready to start trying again.

16th April 1979.

Sometimes I do wonder if One Flew Over the Cuckoo's Nest is not so far from the truth, even in these days of the modern mental hospital. I am having a running battle at the moment with one of the consultant psychiatrists and his registrar, over their use of Abreaction.

Abreaction has its origins in psychoanalysis, where it means the discharge of emotion attached to a previously repressed experience. However, the term was extended to include the use of drugs (such as sodium amytal) as an aid in the interviewing of patients. If a patient appeared to be holding back, the drug would loosen his tongue and open things up.

In the context of espionage or crime fiction, this became known as the truth drug. However, there has always been great scepticism about this. These drugs merely increase talking, which could well include lies and fantasy.

In psychiatry, abreaction has been suggested as a tool in diagnosis, and also in the recovery of memories of childhood abuse. However, most psychiatrists have seldom used it, if at all, and it has been gradually declining over the years (18).

Most of the time I have had no strong feelings about the psychiatrists doing abreactions. One of them confessed that he never actually got any results from them, so he didn't quite know why he bothered. I refrained from saying that it was obviously just one of these professional techniques that made him feel like an expert. Although it is obviously a waste of time, I haven't heard of any actual harm being done.

However, there has been a case recently which has made me extremely suspicious. A young man was admitted to the ward after behaving in various stressed and depressed ways at home. His father was very worried about him. The consultant psychiatrist had got a feeling that this young man might be developing schizophrenia, and had brought him into the hospital to be observed and diagnosed.

Fair enough, so far. But the trouble is, psychiatrists can be very anxious not to miss an important diagnosis such as schizophrenia, which is supposed to be their special area of expertise. Not to notice that someone is psychotic would be a professional humiliation. But it is easy to be misled by a feeling or hunch. That would be like a policeman who *just knows* that someone is guilty, but has no evidence.

Professional discipline requires you to find real evidence, for and against.

The consultant was stuck. The young man had stopped behaving abnormally and could not explain why he was in a mental hospital. Perhaps he was covering up, to avoid further incarceration. An abreaction might release the truth. The consultant asked his assistant (registrar) to carry this out.

That is where it all went wrong. The registrar reported that the young man, under the influence of the sodium amytal, confessed to hearing voices. But when I saw the patient and asked him about this, he denied ever having said such a thing, and that he certainly did not hear voices. So the registrar did another abreaction, and I interviewed the patient again, with the same contradictory results.

I just cannot believe that this young man would deny something that he has supposedly confessed (twice), unless his confession was simply drug-intoxicated nonsense which he has forgotten now that he is sober. Surely they cannot stick a life-long label of schizophrenia on him without better evidence than this, and I have written in his case notes to say so. I feel rather nervous about doing so, as such an open challenge to medical authority is like putting your head above the parapet and waiting to have it blown off.

Not that I should have to worry about such things. After all, this is just a good example of the new spirit of multidisciplinary teamwork in action, isn't it? In the old days at Powick, the important people were the Medical Firms (a Consultant for each geographical patch, together with his junior doctors). The Nursing Staff looked after the wards and did the bidding of the doctors. And there were a few hangers-on, such as occupational therapists and psychologists. But now they have all become members of a Team, and the doctors are supposed to listen to the views of non-doctors. Actually, most doctors have always been perfectly reasonable and amenable, but (as in all professions) there are still a few who turn nasty when their authority is challenged.

It did occur to me that I might be doing the psychiatrists a favour in challenging this diagnosis. They ought to be watching their backs at the moment, as I have read about some entirely normal people who have been playing tricks by going round psychiatric clinics getting themselves diagnosed as schizophrenic on the basis of very flimsy bogus evidence (for example saying that they were hearing voices). Their idea was to try to expose psychiatric incompetence.

11th June 1979.

The new government has not long come into power, with Margaret Thatcher as Prime Minister. The managers are telling everyone to sharpen up and be more efficient. See more patients and do them more good. It is difficult to argue with that. I would love to be more efficient, but the institutional culture of the NHS holds everyone back. *This is the way things are done, because this is the way things are done* is the underlying unspoken rule. Whereas my scientific upbringing tells me to question everything, and if something isn't working it should be changed or abolished. Is it only me who thinks this, or is everyone just keeping their mouths shut?

However, there are things in your own practice that you can change, without anyone being offended (mainly because they don't know about it). Ever since I started work in the NHS I have seen the need to adapt what I was taught as a student, largely by the strategy of *cutting corners.* There are those in my profession who would be offended by this, seeing it as a reduction in quality of work. But there are many examples where you can gain a large increase in quantity (e.g. numbers of patients), with only a small reduction in quality. And occasionally the cutting of corners actually forces you to improve your technique in order to regain that quality.

One example of this occurred years ago when I transferred my relaxation therapy on to tape recordings in order to save huge amounts of my time. Another one that I have established recently is the use of short-form tests instead of routinely doing full tests. A lot of psychologists now are against doing any testing at all, on the grounds that it is scientifically invalid for the purposes of psychiatric diagnosis, and that it is just a way in which psychiatrists are trying to keep us in this subservient role. I do largely agree with this, and feel somewhat alone in saying that I actually enjoy testing patients. My only rational argument for carrying on testing is that this is still the only way I can gain access to the inpatients on the wards, and occasionally it does produce some significant information about the patient's mental functioning (especially if they have suffered some brain damage or other impairment).

However, it has long been clear to me that it isn't necessary to do a full battery of tests (taking an hour or two) to achieve this. A shorter selection of tests is usually perfectly adequate, taking maybe no more than twenty minutes. If the results of this are not clear, then you can always do the fuller version. I collected together hundreds of tests that I have done over the years, and did lots of calculations to check that I would have got much the same results from a shorter version. This has enabled me to carry on seeing the same number of patients on the ward, spending less time in testing and more time in conversation.

18th September 1979.

The NHS managers are always talking about efficiency, but there is one example of inefficiency that I cannot do anything about, because the psychiatrists are in the way.

If you suffer from agoraphobia or some other anxiety-related problem, and you have heard that psychologists can now treat this with behavioural or cognitive-behavioural therapy, you might go along to your GP and ask for this. But your GP would tell you that you cannot be referred straight to a psychologist, as you have to be seen by a psychiatrist first. If the psychiatrist agrees, he will refer you to a psychologist.

So by the time I see such a patient, it could be several months later, and they complain about how long it has taken, as if it is my fault. I feel really embarrassed and angry about this system. It is made worse by the psychiatrists and their waiting lists. Some cynical people suspect that medical waiting lists are deliberately lengthened in order to create a demand for private practice. Patients waiting too long for an NHS appointment may pay the same consultant to see him privately and immediately. I have also heard a consultant saying that he feels positively obliged to keep a reasonably lengthy waiting list, because otherwise people would think he was no good. It is possible that he was joking, but I suspect that he has a point.

I would be quite willing to take these patients directly from their GPs, and many GPs would welcome that. They get complaints from the patients not only about the long wait to see the psychiatrist, but also the rudeness and silly questions that they suffer once they get there. However, the psychiatrists have made it plain that they will not tolerate direct referrals to psychologists, so the GPs dare not do it. GPs are at the mercy of consultant psychiatrists when it comes to getting their difficult patients admitted to Newtown, so they can't afford to offend them.

My psychologist colleagues want me to do something about this. I have started by sending a report to District Headquarters about all these issues.

6

WAR

3rd March 1980.

There has still been no reply from District Headquarters to my questions about implementing the Trethowan Report, in particular the issue of whether psychologists can take direct GP referrals. This is not the first time I have noticed that NHS managers simply avoid giving any reply to awkward questions, not even an acknowledgement. Various bits of gossip make me suspect that discussions have taken place behind my back, but nothing has emerged. One of the consultants was heard to say that there will never be direct GP referrals to psychologists. *Over my dead body* was the expression he used.

My department has expanded over the years, from being just myself, to having a staff of four psychologists. On the one hand they clearly want me to sort out this issue, but on the other hand I can't see any diplomatic solutions. The only way forward will mean declaring war, and I feel bad about exposing my colleagues to that. Do they realise that they will be subjected to hostile fire, and they will have to watch their backs? Will my troops let me down? But today one of them said *Why don't we just go ahead and do it?* And that was that. We have decided to start taking referrals from GPs, and will respond to whatever happens.

8th August 1980.

We didn't get very far before being hauled over the coals. One of the other psychologists has been subjected to attacks about his travel expenses, his professional reputation, and it has even been suggested that he is not properly qualified. We have managed to fend off all of these totally unjustified attacks, but it is very wearing, and my colleague is getting very angry. Now the consultants are trying to divide and rule. They are saying to me that it would be all right if it was just myself taking GP referrals, but my colleagues cannot be trusted because they are less qualified and insufficiently experienced. And then they are going to my colleagues and suggesting that I am going over the top and damaging all our career prospects. I think we are all agreed that any chance of reconciliation with the psychiatrists has now gone.

This has all culminated today in a formal enquiry, to which I was summoned as head of department to account for our sins. Actually I think it worked out quite well, as I managed to turn it against the consultants, who had not expected that. The chairman of the enquiry was the senior medical consultant who represents all the doctors in the District. In other words he is a *proper doctor*, bearing in mind that medical and surgical doctors do tend to look down on psychiatrists. And the consultant psychiatrist giving evidence was the *Kindly One*, who is a normal and reasonable person (which means that he has to tread warily with his more dominant colleagues). And there was also the Personnel Officer, whose role was to raise his eyebrows at all these professional shenanigans.

Fortunately none of them had done any real thinking about the issues, whereas I had spent hours preparing my responses. One complaint was that I was failing to attend the consultants' weekly ward meetings. It was fairly easy for me to demonstrate that if I attended all of these meetings, I would spend half my week just sitting doing nothing, listening to the psychiatrists pontificating about their patients. And then I would be referred some patients simply because I was there, and often for no clinical reason. Whereas if they had to seek me out or send a form, they had to think about whether this referral actually had any purpose.

There was a whole list of completely nonsensical complaints, including vague things like the idea that I was lowering the morale of the other psychologists. They withdrew this one almost immediately when I pointed out that my colleagues were very happy that I was now fighting their corner, and that it was the consultant psychiatrists who were causing us to be troubled.

But then they got to the nitty-gritty, the question of us taking GP referrals.

The usual objections had been listed. There was the one about psychologists being contractually employed to assist psychiatrists, rather than going off and doing our own thing with trivial cases of anxiety. It was easy for me to point out that not being able to go to work or even go out of the house, because of something like agoraphobia, was hardly a trivial matter. At this time, we psychologists do have particular expertise in anxiety and phobic problems, and it seems perfectly reasonable that we should do more of that kind of work, freeing up the psychiatrists to spend more time on psychosis and severe depression (where they claim special expertise).

Next there was the medical responsibility argument. It is supposedly dangerous for psychologists to be let loose without medical supervision, because they will fail to spot serious physical conditions such as brain tumours. I had to point out that our patients would still have a doctor, namely their GP, who is supposed to know a little bit about such things. Were the psychiatrists saying that GPs are totally incompetent? And even if the GP missed something, we psychologists are trained in such a way that we ought to be able to suspect the existence of some physical problem, even if we don't know exactly what the medical diagnosis might be. We can always ask the GP to take another look or refer to a psychiatrist!

I couldn't help mentioning the number of times that I had spotted a medical condition, sometimes minor and sometimes serious, that had been missed by the consultant psychiatrist. Unfortunately, this argument doesn't seem to hold any water. It seems that doctors are allowed to make as many mistakes as they like, because they are medically qualified to do so. Whereas psychologists are not allowed even to be correct about any medical matters, because they are not qualified to express such amateur opinions.

Then came the lie. *GPs don't actually want to refer directly to psychologists,* say the consultants. Untrue. The reality is that significant numbers of GPs are mightily offended by the psychiatrists, for all sorts of reasons of their own, and the idea of missing out the psychiatric middleman appeals to them greatly. But they are wary of saying so.

The simple fact is that we have doubled our patient numbers since taking GP referrals, without reducing our attention to psychiatrist referrals. We have coped with this quite easily because the psychiatrists were not actually generating sufficient work for us. I have drawn a chart of our patient numbers for each month over the past year, showing an impressive increase with GP referrals. The meeting seemed particularly impressed with this. At a time when all sections of the NHS are being harangued about improving our work output, I have surely scored a point here.

Having had quite a reasonable reception for all my arguments, simply by suggesting that the consultant psychiatrists are sadly misguided, I decided not to mention suspicions about their ulterior motives. It is difficult not to notice that the consultants behave quite differently in their private practices, where anxious patients who are paying fees are no longer described as trivial cases who should be made to wait. Is it possible that we psychologists are undermining the psychiatrists' business interests by seeing these patients free of charge on the NHS?

Anyway, the outcome of the meeting was that the psychiatrists were told by District Management to sort the matter out as soon as possible. I don't believe they will do this, especially as I learned today that they had been asked to do this previously, and had simply gone silent. One difficulty is that the NHS is still operating a consensus management system, so that it takes just one man, one veto, to block anything. Nonetheless, I have agreed to cease taking GP referrals (a 'moratorium', the District Health Authority calls it) while these discussions are supposedly taking place. I have to show that I am the one who is reasonable and cooperative with management.

There are a number of problems with consensus decision-making. It gives any self-interested minority group a veto over decisions. When decisions do occur, they may have taken an extremely long time. In some cases, consensus may encourage groupthink, a situation in which people modify their opinions to fit in with what they think others want them to think, resulting in a decision that none of them actually agrees with.

Consensus management in the NHS was summed up by the Griffiths Report (1983) in the following way: If Florence Nightingale were carrying her lamp through the corridors in the NHS today, she would almost certainly be searching for the people in charge.

3rd March 1981.

It has all gone boringly quiet. I am beginning to wonder if a *moratorium* is something to do with a *crematorium*. No word from anyone about anything. This is in marked contrast to last year, when there were angry letters flying about everywhere.

I have been amusing myself for a little while by doing a bit of pseudo-linguistic analysis of all the letters from one of the consultant psychiatrists. He writes extremely long sentences, to the point of losing track of what he was talking about at the beginning of the sentence. But the interesting thing is that his sentences grow longer and longer during this exchange of letters, and I could imagine him increasingly puffing himself up like a toad. I speculated that this reflected his increasing anger as he kept on failing to crush me, but then I discovered that toads do this as a defence tactic rather than attack. They try to make themselves look too big to eat. Does this mean that he feels that he is in danger from *me*, rather than the other way round?

The consultants could never admit to that, of course. Their stance is that I am attempting to transgress against the rightfully established order. They go around saying that I have *declared UDI*. This is a popular expression derived from political events in Rhodesia over the past fifteen years.

The Unilateral Declaration of Independence of Rhodesia from the United Kingdom was enacted in 1965 by Ian Smith, the Rhodesian prime minister. Smith and his party, the Rhodesian Front, opposed black majority rule. The British government, the Commonwealth and the United Nations condemned UDI as illegal. After years of sanctions and other pressures, Rhodesia reverted temporarily to British rule in 1979, before achieving independence as Zimbabwe in 1980.

I might have the same surname as Ian Smith, but I think the UDI analogy, when applied to me, is actually in the opposite direction. The consultants seem to be blind to the fact that the tide has turned against them. It is now official NHS policy that clinical psychologists should achieve professional and managerial independence from psychiatry. That doesn't mean that we should cease to work together, just that psychologists should stop working *for* psychiatrists.

So in fact it is these consultants who have declared UDI. They are refusing to go along with what the rest of the world thinks. Possibly they don't actually realise how many people (including other psychiatrists) disagree with them. Locally they are such dominant characters that no one dares, or can be bothered, to speak to them frankly.

Is anyone going to step forward and bring this to an end?

20th May 1981.

I'm impressed. Somebody in District management has come up with the idea of calling in the Health Advisory Service.

The Health Advisory Service was created in 1969, at a time of increasing anxiety and political embarrassment about the quality of long term care being given to elderly, mentally ill, and mentally handicapped patients in England and Wales. The trigger was the Ely Hospital scandal of 1967, which demonstrated how ill-treatment could be known about but still not reported to those in charge of the NHS. There was clearly a need for an independent body to advise the Secretary of State, and the concept of multidisciplinary review by external professionals was established.

In 1976 the remit of the HAS was widened to include community health and social services. HAS reports are intended to provide useful and constructive guidance to local managers and clinical staff, but there is still also a direct line to government ministers. Advice is offered simply as the combined view of a multidisciplinary group of widely experienced professional people with no axe to grind, unencumbered by local history and politics. The specific advice can be disregarded, but the problems revealed should be tackled in some other way and not ignored. A visit is often the opportunity to examine long-nurtured local grievances in an objective way.

In the early 1980s, HAS reports frequently expressed the view that psychiatry is essentially a community specialty. The discipline is no longer bounded by the hospital perimeter, but reaches out to treat and support most of its patients in or close to their homes. This does not diminish the specialty of psychiatry, but neither does it prevent GPs from choosing to refer to alternative professionals.

Some psychiatrists of course expressed much resentment at this perceived interference, and accused the HAS of being a centralised and costly bureaucracy, running wild with a ill-defined remit. The HAS rejected these criticisms as fallacies, and suggested that they betrayed the prejudices of this minority of psychiatrists (19).

Since that time, the HAS evolved into the Health and Social Care Advisory Service (HASCAS), and is now an entirely independent organisation. It still works in all aspects of mental health and older people's services.

The HAS arrived bright and early this morning to check us out. It was just a two-man team, a psychologist and a psychiatrist, appropriately enough. The psychologist was Bernard Kat, someone we had not met before. The psychiatrist was a Dr. Rogers, who very quickly gave out the impression of being a reasonable man. This was fortunate, as I am now completely traumatised by our local consultants and rather inclined to view all psychiatrists as incarnations of Satan.

Their questions were the usual ones, to which I gave the usual answers. Then they expressed their puzzlement at the fact that there was a problem. Suddenly I felt a breath of fresh air, having lived for so long with the local assumption that all these issues are completely tangled up and insoluble. *Yes, why indeed is there a problem?*

Encouraged to speak frankly, I pulled out a copy of an article written by one of the consultants, in which he describes his view of the role of a psychiatrist as leader of the mental health team. He writes that an important aspect involves monitoring sexual relationships between team members. Surely this is a joke, but actually there is no hint of humour. He does express himself very badly sometimes, but I won't make his excuses for him. *Don't you think that's really weird?*, I suggested. No need to say more. That is why there is a problem.

7th July 1981.

We seem to have actually won this war. I have been a bit reluctant to believe this, as everyone is trying to pretend that nothing has happened. It doesn't help that we are not allowed to see the HAS report. I was grumbling one day about this apparent lack of result, and in the end the administrator had to put me straight. *Some people don't seem to know when they have won*, he said.

It seems that the HAS have recommended that the management of the psychologists should be taken out of the hands of the psychiatrists, and that a District Psychology Service should be set up. They could see nothing wrong with taking direct GP referrals.

Until I know exactly what is going to happen, I remain somewhat wary.

14th July 1981.

One of the consultants announced today that he was going to allow the Community Psychiatric Nurses on his team to take direct referrals from GPs, *in view of what has happened with the psychologists.* That was an outcome I had not been expecting, or even thought about. Excellent. Most of the CPNs are too busy to want any extra work, but they might like to have the principle in place for the future. Like clinical psychology, the CPNs need to win their professional independence. If I have accidentally helped to knock down some of the obstacles to this, it makes our struggles even more worthwhile.

The role of the Community Psychiatric Nurse during the 1960s and 1970s was to provide follow-up and aftercare for people with schizophrenia. Depot medications (long-acting injections) were administered by CPNs to try to prevent relapse. This early role has now diversified, and they have developed an increasing association with Primary Care. An overlap in the function of CPNs, social workers, health visitors, district nurses, psychologists and counsellors has often been noted. CPNs have increasingly provided counselling and cognitive behavioural therapy in general practice surgeries or health centres.

7

FREE AT LAST

19th August 1981.

The Health Authority has followed the advice of the HAS report, and we have been given to the District Medical Officer (poor man!). This is Dr. Ferrer, whose job is to advise the District Health Authority about all medical and clinical services, and we more or less fit into that. We are now officially the District Psychology Service, rather than the Newtown Hospital psychologists.

Dr. Ferrer is a nice man, very helpful. Why am I now so surprised when I find that people are perfectly reasonable? Of course, he too has experienced his fair share of battering by medics, who all want him to do their bidding, whereas his job is to try to find a more balanced view on behalf of the taxpayer.

Another District Medical Officer wrote an article (20) giving the view that the medical profession has seemed too arrogant in the past. They have assumed that medical advice is always more important than advice from others, being not only right but of course always in the best interests of patients.

Health Authorities and the general public are looking for balanced, considered medical views, and sometimes they do get good solid technical or professional information and advice. But often they are given anecdotal evidence and unsubstantiated impressions (described as clinical experience), and also medical politics ranging from national or specialty in-fighting to local opposition to change.

Add to this an ill-advised tendency to support other doctors, not because of the soundness of their case but simply because they are doctors, and it is perhaps remarkable that medical advice is taken as often as it is.

For the moment we are still at Newtown Hospital, in our previous offices, but Dr. Ferrer has given us a secretary (and typewriter) of our own, and we are no longer ruled by the psychiatrists. I get the uneasy feeling that this is just a temporary arrangement while the NHS undergoes further management upheavals.

22nd September 1981.

When our secretary was appointed, we had to confess to her that she was our first, and therefore we were not too clear what she would be doing. Previously, we have simply asked one of the consultant psychiatrists' secretaries to do some typing, and occasionally they would take a telephone message. These secretaries were always busy doing work for all their doctors, so we tried not to bother them too much. Whereas now we have to find enough work to keep this lady busy for the whole morning every morning.

Actually, that has not been a problem. The secretarial work soon expanded to fill the hours available. And even if it hadn't, there is clearly a valuable role for a secretary as someone to chat to, intermittently during the morning. I find her useful as a kind of reality-check. After talking to either psychiatrists or patients, or indeed other psychologists, I need a little bit of normality.

The usual time for a chat is when we make ourselves a cup of coffee in her office. We are fully equipped with a kettle and assorted mugs, and of course a jar of instant coffee. I read somewhere a humorous comment about a department's coffee arrangements being a true guide to its management and organisation, and the truth of this has now dawned on me. The question is: *Who buys the coffee?*

There are an awful lot of possibilities here. Up until now I have done the easiest thing. As the highest paid psychologist, who also drinks more coffee than anyone else, it seems reasonable for me to go to the shop and buy a jar for the department. There are some people who would use advanced management skills to make other arrangements, of course. You could try requisitioning coffee supplies from NHS stores (but you would probably get a huge tin of dreadful powder). Or you could negotiate a petty cash budget, and buy a jar out of that (but you might have to disguise it as postage stamps or something). Or everyone could put ten pence in a tin for each coffee that they had, and new supplies would be bought out of that (but you end up with rather a lot of coins, and some people forget to pay). Or each person could bring in their own favourite brand of coffee with their name on it (needs a large area for jars, and looks very petty). Or you could give up and use the commercial coffee machine downstairs in the main corridor.

I still think that it is much easier if I just carry on buying the coffee, but we now have a secretary who used to work in a large office with one of these other complicated arrangements. She is a conscientious person, and feels it isn't fair on me. So she is being independent and bringing in her own coffee. The rest of us are continuing as before.

17th August 1982.

I have been too busy to write much in the diary this year. We started seeing GP referrals, often at their local health centres, and this has flourished almost more than we can handle. And I have had to spend a lot of time writing management reports and trying to understand what is going on at District Headquarters. I am acting as Head of the District Psychology Service, but really they have not got around to appointing a District Psychologist yet. Everybody thinks that I want this job, after having fought for a District Service, but I am not so sure.

One of the many reasons for my hesitation is that Mrs. Thatcher and her government are beginning to get up steam. Many people in the NHS are getting the impression that our very existence is going to be questioned in monetary terms. Are we too expensive, and should we be privatised or made redundant? These are questions that are shocking to anyone brought up with the old traditions of the British National Health Service. I can see some possible merit, and even excitement, in these issues if tackled rationally, but probably they will become crude ideology. We will be used as a political football. I didn't come into clinical psychology to be a manager, especially on behalf of the Thatcher government.

11th April 1983.

We have our first District Psychologist (Head of Psychology Services, Worcester District). It isn't me, thank goodness. I was nervous of accidentally making myself redundant by not applying for it, so I filled in a form with brief details and then wrote a letter saying I didn't want it! They held the interviews on a Sunday morning, apparently to prevent us from meeting the candidates. Perhaps they thought we would put them off by telling tales about all the goings-on in Worcester in the past few years.

I have considered whether to make a fresh start with a job elsewhere, but my wife would miss her family in this area. Besides, I want to stay around and see what happens next. If you keep moving from job to job, you never know whether things have changed or whether it is simply a change of place.

Our new boss, Peter, has great plans for expansion of the department, doubling it in size in order to provide further specialist psychology services as proposed in the Trethowan report. As well as Primary Care, we will have psychologists working with the elderly, children, general health, and neurology. And general psychiatry, of course. He says that he discussed all this when he was being appointed, and the District managers agreed to it. We can scarcely believe it. Seriously, though, I find it difficult to believe that we will expand so rapidly at this time when all the talk is of cuts in the NHS generally.

15th February 1984.

Maybe I can give myself more time for all these GP referrals if I give up my health psychology work. One of the new psychologists is interested in developing this new specialty. Actually Health Psychology is a bit of a grand name for the fact that I have been getting a steady trickle of patients with Irritable Bowel Syndrome from the gastroenterologist at the general hospital. I have been doing this for several years now, and strangely enough the psychiatrists never had any objection to this particular breach of their defences. Perhaps it was because the gastroenterologist is a medical consultant. Or perhaps the psychiatrists have no interest in irritable bowels.

Irritable Bowel Syndrome (IBS) is a long-term condition that causes recurring pain or discomfort in the abdomen, and a variable bowel habit. It is one of the most common problems of the digestive system, and about one in six people in the UK have at least occasional symptoms. For some people it seriously affects the quality of their life, as the pain or unpredictability of bowel movement interferes with your ability to work or even go out.

The cause of IBS is unknown, and may be some combination of multiple factors. However, there are treatments which help to reduce the symptoms. Attention to diet can be useful. If you get diarrhoea, avoid too much tea, coffee, alcohol and spices. If you are constipated, try increasing fibre such as bran, fruit and vegetables.

If stress seems to trigger the IBS symptoms, it is worth practising relaxation techniques and taking regular exercise. If there are particular psychological difficulties in your life, some sessions with a cognitive behavioural therapist might help.

The gastroenterologist refers these patients to me for relaxation training and stress management, but I have learned the value of also looking at their eating and drinking habits. Indeed I now take a look at these aspects of all my other patients, even those who aren't complaining of any physical symptoms. It is surprising how many of them have quite extreme habits, like twenty cups of coffee per day, or five sugars in each cup, or three litres of neat fruit juice per day. In contrast, some of them drink only two cupfuls of fluid per day, which is supposedly physically impossible, but they insist that this is truly all they have. I am collecting data on all this.

This is quite an interesting development of my clinical

ideas. Previously I assumed that I was restricted to looking at things in purely psychological terms. But this is too narrow. And when psychiatrists diagnose certain conditions as *psychosomatic*, there may be an insulting implication that such patients are *malingering*. The psychiatric (or psychoanalytic) theory that their illness is manufactured, either consciously or unconsciously, is an interesting and entertaining one, but it doesn't often help the patient. Indeed they react badly because they are upset by apparently being accused of *putting it on*. Therefore I have been inclined to dismiss psychological approaches to mystery illnesses, preferring to think that these patients actually do have a physical disorder which has not yet been identified.

However, I am now attracted by the cognitive-behavioural concept of *vicious circles*. I am familiar with this in connection with anxiety problems, for example (where people get anxious about the symptoms of anxiety). It is easy to extend it to some physical problems, because people obviously get anxious (or depressed) about their physical symptoms, and this psychological reaction could add to the effects of the original disorder.

It occurs to me that I have become independent of the psychiatrists not just in a managerial sense, but also in adopting clinical ideas and approaches that they would have belittled. If I had told them that I was asking patients about their dietary habits, for example, I would have been accused of getting into quack medicine. But now I don't have to look over my shoulder any more!

There can be all sorts of connections between mind and body. For example, peptic ulcer was once thought of as being purely caused by stress, until it was discovered to be largely due to a bacterium (Helicobacter pylori). Antibiotic treatment relieves these ulcers. But then it was realised that most people with this infection haven't actually developed ulcers. So there is still a possibility that stress adds to the infection in some way.

The expanding field of Health Psychology (Behavioural Medicine) is now exploring a wide range of health issues and conditions, gaining a better understanding of how biology, behaviour and social context influence health and illness.

13th March 1985.

Just as I was feeling that things are going too well, there is now a huge black cloud on the horizon. The government has introduced even more changes by implementing the Griffiths Report, which introduces *general management* into the NHS. Managers who used to be called *administrators* are now given business titles like *chief executive*.

While this could be a good move (it is time that someone did take charge of the NHS), there is a widespread cynicism amongst clinicians that it is all largely phoney, a way of increasing the numbers of managers (and their salaries).

The Griffiths Report (21) was produced by a team led by Roy Griffiths, whose usual job was Deputy Chairman and Managing Director of Sainsbury's supermarket business (which led to some satirical accusations that he regarded the process of delivering health care as no different to selling tins of baked beans). It is often mentioned that his report was very short (only 25 pages), compared with the usual civil service documents, which was alleged to demonstrate his more business-like approach.

His recommendations were actually perfectly reasonable in themselves, and any difficulties would arise later in the manner of their application. General managers (some coming from businesses outside the NHS) were to be appointed. Budgets would be introduced, together with greater financial accountability. Value for money audits would attempt to make savings, to be put back into patient services. And management training would be increased, especially for doctors. Further, patients were to be regarded as consumers or customers of the business. And customers need to be satisfied. This was a major challenge to the culture in the NHS which regarded standards and outcomes as entirely the preserve of the healthcare professionals.

We had a bit of a panic when they were thinking of putting us back under the same general manager as the psychiatrists. But in the end we were put in the Community Health unit, still safe. Then we were shaken by an apparent threat to make all the psychologists redundant. For some reason this story appeared in the local newspaper, which was complete news to us. Peter tells us that there is no basis to the story, and he has no idea where it came from. However, the story has not been retracted, and the local population is presumably now under the impression that we have all moved away or gone private.

Then I heard that my job in particular was under consideration for redundancy. It turned out that Peter had been persuaded by the Chief Executive to do a management exercise to see how he could make a certain percentage saving on his budget. All departments were doing likewise. Being the most senior (apart from Peter), with the highest salary, my job would obviously save the most. This was a purely theoretical exercise, of course, but why do it (and be found out doing it) if it wasn't going to happen?

At the same time, Peter is being faced with the fact that all the remaining extra psychologists that he had been promised are not going to be funded. This would provide the fictional savings that were being required by the government. Peter now looks very glum, and has announced that he is looking for a job elsewhere. I am not sure whether this is a management failure or a management success.

Somehow I don't think they are that clever, even though there is a lot of impressive-sounding Management Speak being spouted. There is a growing tide of cynicism about this business language. Why does it so often mean the opposite of what it says? The following is a small selection of well known examples:

Management Speak: Business jargon, too often used to spin negative situations so that they might appear more positive.

Action Plan: Back-covering exercise, often in the form of a long and deliberately vague document.

Best Practice: Procedure suggested by an inexperienced committee.

Clinical Governance: Means whatever you want it to mean.

Closure: Evading responsibility by drawing a line under an issue.

Consensus: An imposed management line.

Customer: A patient with no choice other than that offered by the NHS.

Dialogue: Mainly one-way conversation.

Empowering: Tricking an innocent and hard-working subordinate into taking responsibility for your mistakes.

Flagship: Best of a bad bunch.

Flexibility: You have to do it whether you want to or not.

Human Resources: A bulk commodity, like tins of beans.

I Hear What You Say: But I'm not listening.

Interesting: I disagree.

Key Performance Indicator: Arbitrarily chosen statistic.

Marketing approach: Put ethics to one side.

Mission Statement: A long document signifying nothing.

Moving On: Hiding, ignoring or refusing to accept mistakes.

My Door Is Always Open: Now get lost.

On Hold: We have put a stop to it.

Opportunity: A big problem.

Proactive: Putting paper in the photocopier without being told. But genuinely proactive staff are a threat to management.

Under Serious Consideration: We are waiting for the furore to die down before we stop pretending to do something.

Unfit for Purpose: Blame the previous manager.

8

PRIMARY CARE

15th October 1985.

I am seeing GP referrals full-time now, and I'm just beginning to get used to calling it Primary Care Psychology. This is another bit of Management Speak which doesn't roll easily off the tongue. Besides, it is the GP who is Primary, and a referral to me makes me Secondary, surely. When the referrals came from a psychiatrist, they were Tertiary, I presume.

Having said that, I would like to think that occasionally a patient could contact me direct (if they know how). I could always send them to their GP if there might be a medical problem. However, I am not sure whether management will let me get away with that. Their forms probably don't have an appropriate box to tick. What I should be able to do quite easily, though, is to allow patients to come straight back to me if I have seen them previously.

29th October 1985.

It is wonderful having my office at Seaford Court Lodge in Malvern. I always used to say that my dream would be to see my patients in a little old house in town somewhere, meaning the complete opposite to a mental hospital. And here I am!

Peter did achieve several important things in his short time as District Psychologist, and one of them was the acquisition of this house for the Community members of the psychology department. It was going spare, having been bought by the Health Authority, along with the empty old school next door, as a site for the new Malvern Community Hospital. There doesn't seem much chance of the hospital being built for many years yet, if at all, so we should be left in peace. The other psychologists here deal with children and learning disability, while those dealing with psychiatry, neurology and the elderly remain at Newtown Hospital.

As I sit at my desk, I can keep an eye on the goings-on at the Temperance Fountain on the common across the road. This is a drinking fountain dating from 1900, having been erected by the British Women's Temperance Association. It does produce some water, and various passers-by (not all of them children) like to mess about with it. Splashing water over yourself is apparently quite pleasant when climbing the hill on a hot day!

Seaford Court School, facing Malvern Link Common, was chosen as the new Malvern hospital site in the late 1970s. In 1980 it was finally purchased by the West Midlands Health Authority, which said that work would start two years later. But in 1982 the scheme was postponed because of financial cutbacks, and in 1983 it was shelved indefinitely in favour of building a new District General Hospital in Worcester.

Over the years the building became more derelict, and the site more overgrown, although the surrounding parts (including the Lodge) were kept in good order. A number of applications were made in the mid-1990s, both by developers and the Health Authority itself, to raze the site and build housing. These were resisted by Malvern Hills District Council.

Then in 2007 the government announced money for the new hospital, and building commenced at Seaford Court in 2009.

11th February 1986.

One key thing in Primary Care is that you really cannot have a waiting list. You can't afford to start a waiting list, even temporarily, because your workload will be out of control in no time.

My colleague is unfortunately a good example of how this can go horribly wrong. He is a very helpful person and popular with the GPs, so he gets large numbers of referrals. The problem is, his therapy style leans towards psychotherapy and counselling, which can be rather long-winded, as opposed to cognitive behavioural therapy, which can be abbreviated more easily. He also feels conscientiously obliged to see patients for as long as it takes for them to get better, which can take many months or even years. Whereas I am more willing to take a chance and let patients go when they are simply heading in the right direction (providing that they can come back if this doesn't work out).

My colleague's strategy might be all right in private practice, where you can see a limited number of patients for as long as they are prepared to pay the fees. But in the NHS we are supposed to be helping a much wider section of the community. His waiting list has already grown to over a year, and I fear that his only way out of this impasse will be to abandon ship and find a job more suited to his style.

I have never had a waiting list. Perhaps it's because I'm the sort of person who likes to clear my desk at the end of every day, rather than letting things pile up. But also I am very aware that our patients are anxious worriers, and if I were in that position myself I would hate to be kept waiting for months.

Obviously my work capacity has a limit, and I really cannot cope with seeing many more than 25 patients per week (an hour each plus report writing and other tasks). So if I have 50 patients, they have to be seen fortnightly rather than weekly. And if I am being referred 10 new patients every week, I have to say goodbye to 10 patients per week. Simple, really, but you have to be ruthless. I realise that this could end up by seeing each patient only once, which would not be very good, but fortunately it hasn't come to that yet. My only comfort then would be that I always feel that patients benefit most from the first meeting.

Years later in 2008, the waiting list issue has still not been resolved generally. A report by a group of mental health charities (22) complains that the lives of people stuck on long NHS waiting lists for psychological treatments are being damaged as a result. Mental health problems can worsen, relationships can break down, and some people are forced to take time off work (or even give up their jobs).

The report recommends that psychological therapy should be available when needed urgently, within 3-10 days. Therapy services need to be flexible, offering weekend and evening appointments for those who work during the day.

5th August 1986.

If you haven't enough psychologists, maybe you can train and encourage the patients to be their own therapists. Self-help saves a lot of professional time, and in any case it is a necessary element even when having expert therapy. All that the professional does is to point the patient in the right direction. Different problems and different people will require different amounts of guidance, of course, but the more you can harness the person's own efforts the better the result should be.

I am writing a little collection of booklets about common problems such as anxiety, depression, stress and obsessions, for patients to take home to remind them about basic principles. On the back of each booklet I can jot down a list of specific tasks (homework) for the individual patient. This will focus both our minds on producing practical strategies and solutions, rather than just vaguely chatting.

20th May 1987.

There is an awful lot of management stuff going on, new jargon to learn (or laugh at), and piles of really boring documents to read just in case they mean something. I am beginning to realise that this is largely a waste of time as far as I am concerned. This is just the managers playing games amongst themselves, trying to look as if they and the government know what they are doing.

Perhaps I should stand back from it all, and simply get on with my clinical work. There is probably no choice anyway. The managers are too busy managing management to pay any attention to managing clinical matters.

In 1987 we had no idea that this was merely the start of it. From 1974 to 2006 (and beyond) the NHS was in an almost continuous state of what some have called Redisorganisation. Of course, organisations of all types are restructured on a regular basis, but the scale and frequency of it in the NHS has been exceptional. Often each wave of reorganisation has started before full implementation of the previous wave.

The reason usually given is that change is necessary to improve services, supposedly by reducing management costs and increasing patient care. However, other reasons might be to do with a new political party or new minister trying to establish power. There seems to be a cyclical pattern of oscillations between centralisation and decentralisation.

Reorganisation is at best a distraction, and at worst a destroyer of confidence. When organisations decentralise, there is a desperate search for new managerial talent to fill expanded structures. Conversely, when there is centralisation there is a surfeit of well paid staff, some of whom have been promoted beyond their competence. The process of staff reapplying for jobs is slow and draining.

There is a strong argument that the financial unintended consequences of reorganisations often outweigh any beneficial results. It would be desirable to have more stability in health and social care.

17th September 1987.

Dealing with NHS management stuff gives me all the negative emotions: bafflement, paranoia, disgust, fear, depression, anger, hate, helplessness and hopelessness. Seeing patients makes me feel much better. Even when I feel sad or horrified by their experiences, at least it is a straightforward normal emotion about a real human situation.

That young lady Rachel, who came to the clinic this afternoon, seems to be improving nicely after seeing her a few times, which is very satisfying. Originally she was getting panic attacks when sitting at home on her own minding the baby, especially when her husband was out. Her heart would start thumping, and this would lead to her shaking and eventually weeping with fear.

She had gone to her GP, who had tried to reassure her that she had no physical illness and would not collapse or die from these symptoms. No, she wasn't going to have a heart attack. He gave her some tranquillizers to be taken in the event of a panic attack, and referred her to me.

She was grateful to be seen within a few days, and told me that there hadn't been any panic attacks since seeing the doctor, but she was on edge all the time. And now she was worrying about the pills.

Lots of patients worry about taking pills, but Rachel had a special reason to be anxious. During childhood she had lived with her mother in a small flat, her father having abandoned them. But then her mother developed cancer and became chronically anxious. Rachel still has vivid memories of living with a mother who was always worrying and taking increasing numbers of tranquillizers. Consequently when she experienced her first panic attack recently, she feared she was going to be like her mother, and it had brought back a lot of traumatic memories.

Her mother had died when Rachel was only 16, and Rachel had carried on living on her own in the flat. She left school and got a job as a waitress in a restaurant, and eventually she found a boyfriend, who moved in with her. A year ago she had a baby boy, and the events of her own childhood had started coming back to haunt her. What would happen to her baby if she died during one of these panic attacks? Would her boyfriend take him on? Rachel's own father had simply walked away from his responsibilities. Was this what men did? She decided that she and her boyfriend should get properly married, to reassure her about his commitment to the baby in the event of her death.

But soon after the wedding, a friend of hers was killed in a road accident, and this brought back her worries about dying. In addition she started to feel guilty about having upset her mother sometimes by being a horrible teenager. All the bad things she had ever done came back into her mind. Was she now suffering retribution?

Normally she was an active person with plenty to distract her from such thoughts, but when she was a bit bored and idle while baby minding, this was when all her emotion surfaced together with the panic attacks.

After telling me the story of her childhood, she was more able to stand back and come to terms with it. She practised the relaxation and slow breathing exercises, to give her some control over the panic attacks and also to learn to be calm and still while doing nothing.

This seems to have done the trick, and she hasn't needed to take any of the prescribed tranquillizers, which pleased her even more. And me too.

Benzodiazepine tranquillizers were a big media scare in the 1980's. In the 1950's there had been a previous scare, less well publicised, about earlier types of tranquillizer, such as barbiturates. It had been realised that barbiturates could quickly produce a physical addiction, and were also very risky in overdose.

When the Benzodiazepines (Librium, Valium and eventually many others) came along in the early 1960s, they were hailed as being safe, non-addictive, and less risky in overdose. They were very effective in suppressing anxiety symptoms, and most people thought they were wonderful.

Psychological therapists did point out that patients still had to sort out their problems, and that drugs simply helped them feel better while doing so. However it was commonly held that a combination of drugs and psychological therapy would be better than either alone.

But it only took a few years before doctors started to notice a problem. When patients improved, they were supposed to stop taking the tranquillizers. Unfortunately, significant numbers of them became worse again, and required further prescriptions. The doctors then assumed that these anxiety disorders must need longer term treatment, and simply carried on giving out the pills. In fact the patients had become addicted to the benzodiazepines, and were now getting withdrawal symptoms which resembled anxiety.

After several years during which doctors and the pharmaceutical industry were in denial about this, the problem was eventually admitted, and this was widely publicised as a scandal.

In an attempt to retrieve the situation, the medical and pharmaceutical authorities issued advice that benzodiazepines should not be taken for more than four weeks, and should be withdrawn gradually. They are still recommended for short term relief from acute episodes of anxiety.

Subsequently, the number of prescriptions have more than halved in the past 20 years, but remain higher than might be expected. And there is a suspicion that they have simply been replaced with prescriptions for other drugs, such as antidepressants, which may have problems of their own.

The demand for drugs will always be high, even when subject to scare stories, because there is an understandable wish for a rapid relief from extremely unpleasant symptoms. Drug treatment is easily available and cheap. No specialist is required, and GPs can hand it out in five minutes. Whereas psychological therapy, or even simple counselling, can be very hard to come by for the large numbers of people who suffer from these problems.

14th April 1988.

For a long time now, I have been too busy to do any research. I am the only one of my colleagues now who has much belief in the scientist-practitioner model of clinical psychology. We are too busy being therapists and grappling with the politics of the NHS, to spend any time on research. By research, I don't mean just looking things up. I mean doing properly designed experiments and statistical analysis of data that we have collected.

This is a shame, because that is why I came into psychology in the first place, to try to discover things by scientific methods. Until you properly establish whether treatments work, and preferably also how they work, you are really just thrashing around in the dark. When you treat patients blindly, you might even be doing them harm. In psychology, it is too easy just to make things up or follow other people's opinions. You need a scientific approach to gather objective evidence.

For example there is a popular idea that too much coffee is bad for all sorts of aspects of your health. It is said to causing insomnia or anxiety, for example. You could just tell patients to stop drinking coffee, but really that isn't good enough. So I have been enquiring about their consumption of coffee and tea, working out how much caffeine it amounts to, and then asking them to reduce as much as they can (but not totally, in case of withdrawal symptoms). And I have been scoring how severe their symptoms are, before and after reducing the caffeine. Admittedly, this is not a foolproof scientific design, but it might give some idea about what happens.

The results seemed fairly plausible. The patients who drank a lot of coffee improved most if they reduced the coffee by at least 6 cups per day. It helped their anxiety, irritability, sleep problems, headaches, or IBS. Those who failed to reduce much did not improve so much. I am deducing from this that there is no point in telling people to reduce their coffee unless they are having at least 6 cups per day, and they have to reduce by 6 cups in order to make a difference.

Given that my scientific methodology is a little shaky, I was doubtful whether I would get this published, but one of the BPS journals has taken it (23). That is very pleasing and encouraging.

The Scientist-Practitioner model goes back particularly to the 1949

Boulder (Colorado) Conference on Graduate Education in Clinical Psychology. Its basic principles are as follows: Using tests and therapies which follow scientifically-based protocols. Seeking out published scientific findings to apply to your work. Framing and testing hypotheses as part of your normal style of work. Working with other professions to encourage the delivery of scientifically-based healthcare. Contributing to practice-based research and development.

Some have questioned if it is possible, in today's climate, to continue to expect clinical psychologists to adhere to this model. Many clinicians cannot find the time to complete their practical duties, let alone conduct research or remain up-to-date with cutting edge science. Nevertheless, the scientific-practitioner model remains highly valued by most members of the profession, even if reality falls somewhat short (24).

23rd February 1989.

It isn't just the psychologist who should try to work scientifically. Some patients have problems which are good examples of non-scientific styles of thinking. When someone has a belief or a suspicion which worries them, they make the mistake of following the strength of their feelings rather than seeking objective evidence and weighing this properly.

Jealousy problems are an example of this. I have been seeing quite a few of these recently. It's not something I have dealt with much before, so I have been looking it up to try to clarify my thoughts.

The experience of jealousy is a complex one, involving a fear of loss, suspicion or anger about betrayal, low self-esteem and sadness, uncertainty and loneliness, a particular fear of losing someone to a rival, and general distrust. It has been described as a cognitively impenetrable state where education and rational belief matter very little.

While jealousy is a common human experience, possibly rooted in a biological instinct to protect our own interests against others, there are also extreme pathological forms of it. If it is combined with a paranoid type of personality disorder, it becomes even less accessible to rational discussion. This sort of person will make continual false accusations against their loved one, no matter how often they are denied and disproved. It may develop into violence, but the verbal and emotional battering is enough on its own to traumatise the other person.

Attempts to treat extreme jealousy can be very tricky, even if the person admits to it in the first place. Some antidepressant medications have been claimed to help, but possibly only as a temporary calming measure. Psychotherapy also has its successes, but it is likely to be difficult. Sometimes the only realistic intervention that a therapist can make is to help the partner (the victim) of the jealous person. Can the victim come to terms with (shrug off) the jealousy, or do they need to escape (dump or divorce)?

The case of this lady today, Joan, has been fairly easy. She is not normally a jealous or paranoid type of person, and her recent problems have been just a bad patch. She and her husband Ian have been married for over 30 years, and they have children and grandchildren.

The trouble started at the Christmas party at her husband's place of work. Wives were invited, of course, and the boss went round making friendly conversation with them all. Unfortunately the boss put his foot in it by mentioning the current office joke about Ian and one of the secretaries. Apparently someone saw humour in the idea that Ian might fancy this secretary, the joke being about the fact that she is very glamorous and rather posh, whereas Ian is a rather simple rustic character. He often gets teased about all sorts of things, and his helpfulness towards this woman provided some ammunition for his workmates.

Listening to the boss, Joan suddenly felt a great fear. Was Ian having an affair? This thought ate away at her for the rest of the evening, and when they got home she launched into an interrogation of him. What was he up to? He protested that he wasn't up to anything, and next day he persuaded his boss to telephone Joan to explain.

Unfortunately Joan didn't understand the joke. She didn't see her husband as rustic and a figure of fun. Why wouldn't another woman want him? She began to see further clues. For many years she had put up with him being a workaholic who went to work at 6 am and came home at 6 pm. He was a helpful soul, never complaining, and always happy at work. But by the time he came home, he was tired and morose. It seemed to Joan that he loved his job more than his wife and family. Now she became gripped by the thought that this other woman was the reason he was always at work.

So she started asking him for answers, over and over again until he didn't know what to say. She searched his pockets and found bits of paper with telephone numbers. When he got out of bed in the morning, she noticed that he looked out of the window in the direction of the town eight miles away where the woman lived. Some evenings she went round to his place of work, spying on him to see if he really was working late.

But he was always where he said he would be, and Joan could find no evidence of an affair. But that didn't stop her worrying, and after weeks of sleepless nights she went to her doctor, who referred her to me. She was now worrying about making Ian's life a misery by checking up on him. I reassured her that it was perfectly reasonable to search for evidence, unlike some people who prefer to carry on being suspicious rather than risk finding out that their suspicions are correct. But after looking for evidence and not finding any, she should draw a line under it.

Instead, I pointed her in the direction of the real problem, namely the fact that Ian spends too much time at work, gets tired, and they don't enjoy any time together.

Joan considered this carefully. She could try to change things, for example by laying down the law and making him come home earlier. However, she predicted that this would cause more trouble than it was worth. He would never change, because he is simply that sort of person. Now that she is clear about this, she can accept him as he is. She has always done so in the past, and will do so again.

To further reduce her tension and improve her sleep, she is exercising by doing more walking instead of taking the car.

9th May 1990.

The NHS is being reorganised again. Instead of being a proper business delivering its services to customers (patients), we are to operate as an *internal market*, going through the motions of selling our services to each other. That means, of course, that our services need to have their costs calculated in some detail, in order that the purchasers (GPs or health authorities) can pay the right price for them.

To that end, we have all been given palmtop computers to record which patients we have seen each day, and for how long, as well as how much time we spend on paperwork. In the past, we might have been given forms to fill in, and we would have called them time sheets. But the managers have grown wise to the horror of having thousands of forms littering their offices. These pocket computers can be downloaded straight on to the main computer at headquarters. Unfortunately the psychology department is not wired to the internet yet, so our secretary has to drive to Worcester with our palmtops once a month to hook them up to the computer. I am making a small protest by recording on my palmtop that it takes half an hour every day to fill in the data.

In 1989 a report called Working for Patients proposed what became known as the Internal Market. Some parts of the NHS would become Providers selling their services to others, the Purchasers. Providers were hospitals or community-based services, who were to become independent Trusts. Purchasers were the Health Authorities, and also any general practitioners (Fundholders) who could be given their own budgets.

Despite widespread opposition from the other political parties, professional bodies, trade unions and the general public, it was pushed through Parliament in 1990 by the large Conservative majority. During the following years, the criticisms continued. The whole NHS became fragmented, with each hospital in competition with the others. Primary and Secondary Care found themselves in an adversarial position. Because of its complexity, it proved to be very expensive, doubling the administrative costs.

I just hope that the GPs don't take all this too seriously. The data that I put into my palmtop will come out at the other end as a price that the GPs have to pay for one of their patients to see me. They might be shocked to see how much I cost. I am now on a Top Grade salary, and in addition there are considerable overheads (the cost of our offices, secretary, equipment, travel, and so on). If they look at that and compare it with the price of some antidepressants, they might decide to give me a miss. Or they might look for some cheaper kind of counselling.

Some of the managers have already started talking about ways of possibly cheating this system. If we see a patient for a long session, more than 20 minutes perhaps, could we count it as two sessions? It would look as if we were seeing twice as many patients. I really can't be bothered with any of that.

21st August 1991.

People seem to be getting very stressed at work, and I don't mean just the NHS.

There seems to be a culture of working longer and longer hours, and some people are blaming this on the culture of the Thatcher government.

Prior to the 1980s, average working hours had been in long-term decline. But then the incidence of long working hours (defined as more than 48 hours per week) increased during the 1990s, although some people's hours were still reducing. By the end of that decade, over a third of men with dependent children were working more than 50 hours per week.

Manual workers are rewarded for long hours by being paid valuable overtime, and they tend to resist any attempt to reduce their hours. Professional and managerial workers see it as a requirement of the job, and believe that it helps their career by demonstrating commitment.

Long hours working is associated with various negative effects, such as decreased productivity, poor performance, physical and mental health problems, and lower motivation.

Colin is one of my more grateful patients, bringing me a packet of biscuits every time I see him. He worked in an engineering factory for many years, doing amazing hours: 7 am to 10 pm, six days per week. He liked having the big wages, and is proud of having paid off his mortgage several years ago. In addition, he had grown to be proud of both his job and the company.

His wife had left him years ago, and then his girlfriend dumped him, complaining about the fact that he was always at work. Just when he was feeling a failure in his personal life, things started to go wrong at work. The company was taken over, and the new managers installed a new computer system. As often happens, it developed serious teething problems, but the managers put the blame on Colin and his colleagues for not using it correctly.

This conflict between managers and staff grew more and more bitter, and Colin took on the role of spokesman for his more junior colleagues. During one particular argument with his boss, Colin was trying to explain that he was upset about his mates getting upset. But the boss twisted this and suggested that Colin must be gay. At that point, Colin lost all hope. How could anyone have a rational discussion with a manager like that?

By then he was unable to sleep at nights because of all these angry thoughts going round and round. He was drinking heavily to try to relax, but then feeling sick and unable to eat. He could not face going to work, and his GP signed him off.

After many discussions with me about his over-conscientiousness, and how it had collided with a pernicious managerial situation in the factory, he realised that it was not possible for him to return to this job. His colleagues were advising him that the factory situation was still the same. He would be hitting his head against a brick wall.

But it made him angry to think that he had been forced out of a good job by these idiot managers. He was going to have to pay for their errors. Fortunately it turned out that he had been in the company pension scheme for many years, and it allowed for early retirement on the grounds of ill-health. His GP and myself signed forms to say that he would be unfit to return to his job for the foreseeable future, and then he was free!

Colin began to feel better almost immediately, and then started to feel guilty about not working, and I have had to restrain him. Perhaps he could get a little part-time job eventually, but first he needs to take it easy and learn to enjoy himself first.

I feel rather good about helping patients to get an early retirement. Teachers are my main customers for this, perhaps because they are lucky enough to have a pension scheme which caters for it. Some people might think that they are just manipulating the system, but the ones I see are clearly genuine. They are usually the over-conscientious sort, who have been struggling on for years, ashamed of how they feel but unwilling to give up.

I must admit that it is nice to have this kind of power. In the old days, official organisations would not take any notice of what psychologists said. Only medical consultants could write reports, sign forms and give opinions. It is another sign of the advancement of the psychology profession that my signature is taken at face value.

I have even been able to argue with insurance companies about the silliness of the out-of date psychiatric diagnosis system that they were using on their forms, and they accepted my opinion!

10th March 1992.

When people do not turn up for their appointments, but don't cancel them either, this has always been a source of irritation for clinical staff. In these days of workload targets, when every minute has a price on it, the irritation is even greater. However,

I suppose this might motivate clinical staff to do what they can to minimise it, by giving better service in some way.

Non-attendance affects all specialties: medicine, surgery, general practice, dentistry, psychiatry and psychology (26). The national average rate of non-attendance typically runs at about 10 per cent of all appointments, which adds up to a staggering amount of time and money. A patient's failure to attend may delay another patient's appointment, and any delays may allow illnesses to worsen.

When surveyed, non-attenders give a wide variety of reasons, or none at all. About a third say they forgot. When a positive effort is put into sending patients reminders and information about how to get to the clinic, there is usually some improvement in non-attendance, but it never disappears. Hospital specialties commonly allow for this simply by overbooking.

I like to think that my patients won't forget, because they never have to wait long enough to do so. I used to think that it would help them to attend if I saw them at their local health centre, so that they don't have to travel so far from the outlying parts of this rural county. However, the non-attendance rate seemed even higher, if anything, and it really did feel a waste of time for me to be hanging about in someone else's office at a Health Centre with nothing much to do. So now all my patients come to my office in Malvern, and they don't seem to mind travelling, especially as there are no parking problems and they could even come by train to the station next door.

There is still some non-attendance, of course, but now I can make use of it as bonus time to do paperwork. Or to have another cup of coffee and a chat to our secretary! You never know why someone did not attend. Sometimes you think that there are patterns of non-attendance which might tell you something. You can go for several weeks without a single failed appointment, and then suddenly one day no one at all turns up (except for your last late evening appointment, of course!). You start to wonder what possible cosmic force has caused them all to forget. But maybe that's just the nature of randomness.

9

BEGINNING OF THE END

25th March 1993.

I have been smoking cigarettes ever since I started at Powick Hospital. In those days, it seemed that everyone smoked and took pleasure in it, whereas now quite a few people have given it up and the remainder are less happy about it. The Health Authority has acquired a no-smoking policy, of course, and NHS staff are supposed to smoke only in designated smoking areas. I have designated my office as a smoking area, on the grounds that it has excellent ventilation (there is a chimney rising from a beautiful Victorian fireplace, and tall French windows leading out on to the veranda).

At home, for years now I have smoked only in the garden and porch, as my wife Margaret is in poor health and has some breathing difficulties from the polio that she suffered as a child. Perhaps I should give up smoking for her sake, although she says she is only worried about its possible effects on me.

But a few weeks ago I had a bit of a shock when I noticed that a small lump had appeared in my groin. After a quick bit of self-diagnosis, I realised that I was developing a hernia. In itself it is nothing to worry about, but I know that sooner or later I will have to go into hospital to get it fixed. How on earth am I going to survive in hospital without smoking? Every day

I get through at least 30 cigarettes, which is one every half an hour. After just a couple of hours without one, my brain turns to jelly. I hadn't thought about it like this before, but now I realise that I am a slave to cigarettes. I am an addict. This is not good. I need to be free.

On the way down the road today, I parked outside some shops, and then noticed the pharmacy. Suddenly I decided to go in and buy a box of nicotine patches. I know nothing about these, really, but I have read something about them and know that this is what I am going to do.

Nicotine is a drug that is inhaled from the tobacco in cigarettes. It gets into the bloodstream from the lungs, and stimulates the brain very quickly. This effect soon dissipates as the blood level of nicotine falls after each cigarette. Then you develop withdrawal symptoms such as restlessness, poor concentration, irritability, and generally feeling awful. So you have another cigarette, and life feels better again. Many smokers would like to stop, but the effects of any prolonged withdrawal (sleeplessness, depression and extreme tension) are so horrible that they give in and start smoking again before there has been enough time for the withdrawal symptoms to wear off. Some luckier people seem to be less addicted and give up fairly easily, but most smokers are truly hooked.

Nicotine Replacement Therapy is a way of getting nicotine into the bloodstream, so that the withdrawal symptoms are lessened and you can stay off cigarettes for long enough to get used to the idea of not smoking. Then the nicotine can be reduced and stopped more easily. It is a way of giving your willpower a chance. NRT does help, especially when combined with professional support and counselling, and possibly with the addition of some antidepressants. However, the success rate is still not brilliant (15 - 30%), and it is clearly better not to start smoking in the first place.

13th April 1993.

The nicotine patches have been magic, up until now. After I stuck the first one on my arm, within an hour I knew that I had no further need for cigarettes. Indeed I gave away my entire stock of two hundred to a relative who could not believe his good fortune. After the first day without smoking (and no problem), I felt jubilant. This was something I had not imagined possible.

After a couple of weeks, I was wondering what to do next, but the instructions simply said to give it a month. But a week later I found myself in a very peculiar state. It was as if I was drunk, with bodily sensations of movement in all directions. This was actually quite pleasant, but obviously not really desirable in the cold light of day. It reminded me of the pleasurable giddiness that I felt when I first learned how to smoke, and I guessed that the patches must have given me an overdose of nicotine. But now after using a lower dose for several days, the strange sensations have persisted, and I am worried that something is wrong. So I have decided to stop using the patches. Perhaps I will be better then, off all nicotine.

20th April 1993.

I am in a bad way. This is cold turkey. My brain is screaming and I cannot sleep. I've got a problem, so I am going to have to give myself some professional advice. Some antidepressants might help the sleep, so I have been to my GP and he has given me the ones I want (my patients recommend them). Also I am going to do some physical exercise, by walking around Malvern every evening (some of the streets are quite a challenge, being on a steep hill).

Many people exercise to reduce weight, with the aim of becoming healthier or more physically attractive. But it is also an extremely effective stress reliever.

Exercise counteracts stress in all sorts of ways. Intense forms of exercise seem to provide an outlet for frustration and anger. Endorphins are produced in your body, giving mood a natural boost. Exercise also functions as a distraction, by focusing your mind on either the activity or the change of scenery. If it helps you feel better or fitter, this will improve your self-esteem. In general, exercise improves your resilience to stress.

17th May 1993.

I soon gave up the antidepressants because I felt even worse. However, my walking is definitely doing the trick. At first I was so unfit that I could only manage half an hour at moderate speed, but soon I noticed that my breathing is so much clearer than when it was clogged by cigarettes. Now I am walking at speed for an hour every evening. Coming home down the hill, I feel as if I could carry on walking for ever. I am soaked in sweat and feeling really good.

I did have a few days off work when it was at its worst, but since then I have just about managed to keep on working. But as each day goes on, and especially in the late afternoon, I feel a strange sort of tension coming on. It originates somewhere behind my nose. I tried to describe it to one of my colleagues. It is as if there is a little man, a demon, sitting just above my nasal cavities, poking my brain. I think he wants a cigarette, but I don't, and he is angry about that.

It is good to observe that I have no inclination whatsoever to have a cigarette. I don't even have to fight against it. Perhaps I know that if I have a cigarette, I will only have to go through all these horrors a second time. Once is bad enough.

6th September 1993.

I am definitely a non-smoker now. I look back in some shame at the things I didn't know before. How the breath smells, for example. The smell of cigarette smoke doesn't bother me, but smokers do have a smell. The other day I saw a patient who had been having a cigarette on his way to my office, knowing that he would not be allowed to smoke on NHS premises. He sat and talked to me for an hour, without smoking, and when he left I suddenly noticed that the air in my office was filled with a haze. I even called my secretary to have a look at this, as I had never noticed such a thing before. Somehow this man had breathed out all these visible fumes.

And how unfit you become if you smoke. I never worried about cancer, which would probably come late in life and save you from years of dementia. But more immediately, smoking hinders your everyday ability to breathe effectively, and I never noticed that until now.

Best of all, I have freedom. I can go anywhere without having to carry cigarettes and a lighter, and without having to arrange my life around my next smoke. It is extraordinary how liberating that is.

12th October 1993.

I am getting very worried about Margaret, but I don't want to worry her by telling her this. We had a big panic three years ago when her breathing went into stridor, presumably due to the fact that her larynx is partially paralysed from her childhood polio. The hospital staff tried to relieve her breathing, but after many hours her airway was becoming totally obstructed, so they had to insert a tube. This was removed the next day when she was settled, and after a few days she came home, seemingly recovered. But maybe the tube had caused some damage, as a week later she found that she could not swallow properly and was at risk of choking. She has always had an understandable fear of choking, as she cannot cough normally to bring anything back up.

Since then she has had to live on nothing but liquid food, in the form of Complan meal replacement. Anything thicker (or indeed thinner) just won't go down. Somehow she has got used to this, but I find it very difficult eating in front of her. At Christmas I have developed a new tradition of eating a quick meal of curry, while she jokes about putting a sprig of holly on her mug of Complan.

Secretly I fear that this is going to end very badly. She asks me if I would marry again if she dies, and I try to pretend that neither of these events is going to happen. If I still smoked, I would go out in the garden for a smoke and some tears, so I just go and sit in the garden anyway.

Poliomyelitis is an infectious disease caused by a virus, and is potentially a serious neurological illness with paralysis which can prove fatal. It is now almost unknown in developed countries, due to highly successful vaccination programmes and other public health measures.

The last polio epidemics in the UK occurred in the 1940s and 1950s, affecting mainly children and young adults. About 30,000 people survived with varying degrees of disability, some mild and some severe. But then about half of them have developed new or worsened disabilities many years later. This is called the Late Effects of Polio, or Post-Polio Syndrome.

Typically the deterioration develops 30 years or more after the original illness, and is not directly related to the age of the patient. There is a debate about whether it is mainly due to complications arising from existing neurological and orthopaedic impairments, or is due to new changes in affected muscles. Is it because of increased wear and tear in a person struggling for years with weak muscles, or do the muscles simply degenerate further anyway?

As well as the limb muscles, those responsible for speech, swallowing and respiration can also be involved. Obstructive sleep apnoeas may arise from problems in the pharynx and larynx. These are characterised by snoring or stridor-like noises during sleep, associated with irregular respiration, waking up un-refreshed, and daytime sleepiness.

The patient with Late Effects of Polio or Post-Polio Syndrome may become anxious and depressed. The appearance of new symptoms brings back traumatic memories of the original illness as a child. Uncertainty about the future becomes a major problem. There is fear about having to cope with further loss of physical function.

23rd November 1993.

Sometimes born-again non-smokers become a bit of a pain by trying to stop everyone else smoking. In my case, I began to complain about the fact that people did not seem to realise how difficult it was to give up smoking. Even I, a professional psychologist who sometimes tried to help patients with this problem, had no idea of how ill you could feel. There used to be a sort of conspiracy of silence about the health risks and addictive nature of tobacco, but now the silence is about the difficulties and health risks of giving it up.

I am particularly scathing about NHS management, who send round over-simplistic memos to say that they will offer support to any member of staff trying to stop smoking. What do they mean, *offer support*? That sounds like Management Speak, the sort of offer that they do not intend anyone to take up. Do they realise that their staff may develop withdrawal symptoms and depression so severe that they may need to take time off work? There are all sorts of risks involved. Is management offering to take responsibility for all that? I don't think so.

It is in the nature of psychological problems that one thing leads to another, for good or ill, and the effects of giving up smoking can be unpredictable. I saw a patient today whose attempts to improve his health could have gone badly wrong. About six months ago, he gave up smoking (unaided, just stopped) but then developed pains or discomfort in his chest and abdomen. He became very preoccupied by his worries about these pains, wondering if they might signal cancer or heart disease. For several months he bottled it all up, not mentioning it even to his wife. Then his sleep became poor, and he was feeling irritable and losing his temper at work (which could have led to losing his job).

Eventually one evening he felt at the end of his tether, thinking that he was about to die. He started remembering a friend who committed suicide a few years ago. At this he burst into tears, and at last he confessed to his wife how he had been feeling. She was extremely alarmed to hear all this, and insisted that he should go and see the doctor. After a thorough examination, the doctor was able to reassure him that there was nothing physically wrong, but maybe the pains were being caused by stress.

When I first saw him, he explained why he had bottled up his worries for so long. His mother is the sort of hypochondriac who complains compulsively about all her aches and pains, and this irritates him a great deal because he gets infected with her worries in turn. He long ago resolved not to be like his mother, so he always keeps his mouth shut about his own worries, even when he should tell someone.

His chest and abdominal pains were fairly easily explained. Being unhealthily health-conscious, he had taken to drinking five pints of fruit juice per day, which can easily produce stomach discomfort. I suggested a reduction and dilution of this juice.

In addition, he confessed that after giving up smoking, he had taken up chewing gum as a new habit. He chewed all day incessantly, and his wife had complained because it irritated her, but it had not occurred to them that it might be irritating his stomach. I suggested that the chewing gum had long ago served its purpose in helping him give up smoking, and he could now afford to give it a rest. His symptoms have improved almost immediately.

The problem with sugar-free chewing gum may arise if there is an artificial sweetener. Some of these can cause minor stomach symptoms such as bloating and cramps, and with large doses there can be diarrhoea and weight loss.

Virtually anything consumed to excess is a possible hazard to health. Quite apart from any consideration of specific food intolerances (a difficult and uncertain area), it is very useful to keep a look out simply for any habitual excesses.

28th January 1994.

I am numb. Margaret died in bed on the morning of New Year's day. I found her lying there looking quite peaceful, and I had to look twice to see what had happened. She had choked on something, maybe saliva or phlegm or reflux, while asleep.

I have been watching her carefully all these years, but somehow she managed to go while my back was turned.

I am still shaking inside, but I did not dare to take more than a week off work. My colleagues said it was too early for me to come back, but I can't afford to let the referrals build up on my desk. I would never catch up. But more immediately, I just need to keep myself going.

It is very hard seeing patients when you are in a state of shock. Fortunately, I have always been quite good at putting on a professional front, either a smile or a poker face. But suddenly I feel that most of my patients' problems are smaller than mine. I long to tell them that *my wife is dead!* Sometimes I get tears in my eyes, and they think that I am feeling sympathetic with their sad story.

Instead of brooding at home in the evening, I go for my long antidepressant walks. Then I can sleep, but not in our bedroom. I can still see her there.

18th May 1994.

I have had my hernia done. When I came round from the anaesthetic I was weeping, and the nurse thought I was in pain. In my semi-conscious haze I managed to explain that actually it was grief.

I had it done in the private hospital rather than go anywhere near the NHS hospital. That was an interesting step for someone who has always believed strongly in the NHS, and disapproves of the social snobbery of private medicine. I just couldn't face going to the shabby old hospital where I had spent so many anxious and miserable hours with Margaret. So I was very pleased with my day and night in a comfortable private room with television and excellent meals. Perhaps the NHS will be like that one day?

After many years of planning and waiting for funding, the new Worcestershire Royal Hospital was opened in 2002, on the site next to the previously new Newtown Hospital. It delivers services previously scattered between three separate sites and replaces buildings going back to the 18th century. The design breaks away from the traditional hospital layout of long narrow buildings, and is fitted with the latest medical equipment. It was funded through the Private Finance Initiative.

On the whole the new hospital is a great improvement, and today I would be happy to have my hernia fixed there. However, there are two regular topics of complaint amongst its patients and visitors. Like many NHS hospitals, there are parking problems, and the meals can be somewhat less than excellent.

10

TIME TO GO

15th March 1995.

I must try to stop feeling so angry with NHS managers. A few days ago, I actually shouted at one over the telephone, and made her cry. It was the middle of the night, and I had been called out by the police because our offices in Seaford Court Lodge had been burgled. So I was already somewhat agitated, and then the policeman said that I should get the Health Authority to do something about making our building secure. We have old wooden window frames and no alarm. *Get the Health Authority to do something about it.* My heart sinks.

The managers have no money for security. They have plenty of money to give us palmtop computers in order to calculate phoney prices to charge GPs for our services. But security is not on the government's list of priorities and targets, so there is no money for that.

I did have one laugh about the burglary, though. The only things taken by the burglar were two of the palmtop computers. Was he going to trade them on some sort of *internal market* between members of the criminal fraternity? Fortunately he was brilliantly caught in the act by a passing policeman, so we have got our palmtops back. I have changed the password on mine to the name of the burglar, as a memorial to this occasion.

Eventually the department was fitted with fortress-like security, at significant cost.

Crime is a financial burden on all parts of society, and the NHS is no exception. In earlier more innocent days, there was an assumption that a public service which helped sick people would be relatively immune to attack by criminals. This perception has changed somewhat in recent years. In 2003 the NHS Security Management Service was set up, to advise and train local staff in tackling these sorts of problems in their areas of work.

13th June 1995.

I really am doing my best to be more relaxed and understanding about NHS managers, but it isn't easy. In their defence, I can see that they are just following orders which ultimately come from the government. Even if they think that these policies are completely potty, they have to carry them out, and in order to try to stay sane they have to try to believe in them.

The thing that has riled me recently has been the gardening services. Around our building there are various lawns, shrubs and trees, and they have to be kept tidy. Originally the NHS employed its own little team of gardeners, who went around their district caring for the green areas around all the clinics and hospitals. And they did it in the old-fashioned, caring and flexible sort of way. But then this was all *contracted out*, supposedly to get better *value for money* (Management Speak for *cheap*).

So every week now a gang of men arrive and set about slaughtering everything in sight, with mowers, blowers and strimmers making a terrific noise. After precisely an hour they climb back in their lorry and disappear. During that hour I cannot hear anything that my patients are saying, so I have asked the manager if they could come at a different time when I am not likely to be seeing anyone. I have also asked why they haven't pruned back the buddleia bush, which grew as a weed and is now spreading over the path to the front door.

The gardeners have helpfully arranged to change their time of arrival, but the manager informs me that they cannot prune the buddleia. Apparently the gardening contract runs from April to September (no gardening needed during the other six months!), and buddleias are supposed to be pruned in February or March (according to the gardening manual). In fact I know very well that there is nothing to stop them being pruned at other times if necessary, but the gardening company is not going to budge. If the NHS is mean enough to give only half a contract, we will get only half a job.

By now I have learned that if you want a job done, you do it yourself. So on Saturday morning I went with my bow saw and cut the buddleia to the ground. No one has mentioned its absence, so I think I will get away with it.

Contracting-out (out-sourcing) has become a widely accepted method of controlling the costs of non-medical services such as cleaning, catering and estates management. In more recent years there has been some movement towards extending this to clinical services of various kinds.

Public service unions have grave doubts about all this. They argue that the NHS has lost control of its contracted out workforce, and there are problems with quality. These jobs have become low paid and thankless, resulting in high turnover and recruitment problems. Previously these staff would have stayed in the NHS for many years and would have had pride in their contribution to patient care.

6th July 1995.

I am fifty years old now, and there was a memo today from the Personnel Department (Human Resources, I should say, but for some reason this always makes me think of meat and cannibalism). The leaflet said that the NHS pension scheme would allow staff aged fifty to retire early, albeit with a reduction in pension. Are they trying to get rid of me? There is still a continual pressure for cuts (*efficiency savings*) to be made, so presumably they would welcome anyone voluntarily abolishing their own salary.

No, not yet, I still have work to do, but maybe I will think again at 55. That's a new thought for me. There was a time, not long ago, when I could not imagine retiring before 65, but now I can see it coming much sooner.

16th January 1996.

I have just read that Professor Trethowan has died. His report on clinical psychology in 1977 was very helpful to the development of the profession, and I was pleased to have actually met him on one occasion when he visited our local day hospital. So I feel quite sad at this news.

His obituary (27) noted that during the 1960s and 1970s he was consultant adviser in psychiatry to the Department of Health, and a member or chairman of various committees. In those days, the obituary observed, the management revolution had yet to erupt. Instead, people like Trethowan were there, senior members of the medical profession, trusted by their colleagues and relied upon to give sound and sensible advice to ministers and civil servants.

9th September 1996.

I seem to be seeing a lot of road accident victims suffering from stress and anxiety.

Maybe the financial pressures of the 1990s are making people rush around too much and too dangerously. Or is it that people are beginning to realise that they can sue for compensation, and the solicitors need a psychologist's report to back them up?

Sometimes these patients seem a bit embarrassed about claiming money for their emotional suffering, but actually they are owed more than just the costs of their car repairs, especially if they were a victim of someone else's bad driving. They should be seeing me anyway for some therapy, and doing a report for their solicitor is a good way of getting them to attend. If they don't need therapy now, they certainly will later on when the other side's solicitors start fighting back and querying their symptoms. This makes the patients burn with anger. I have sometimes warned patients that a legal battle could make them worse, and they have to try to distance themselves from it.

A considerable proportion of road accident victims, whether physically injured or not, suffer from psychological symptoms which may last for months or a year or more. These include general anxiety and depression, post-traumatic symptoms such as horrific memories of the accident, and travel phobias (including worry and anxiety about relatives who are travelling). They may have difficulty going on the roads either as a driver or passenger. Victims who were rendered briefly unconscious and cannot recall the accident are less likely to suffer these kinds of symptoms (28).

14th April 1997.

After listening to the horrors that can suddenly happen to you on the roads, I have been trying to persuade all my patients of the merits of defensive driving. Adjust your position and speed in order to give yourself sufficient time to react to unexpected events.

In discussing this with people, I have been impressed by how many of them are driving in a hurry for reasons to do with stress. None of them mention the simple pleasure of driving fast on an open road. They are all in the grip of the *not enough hours in the day* syndrome. There is the businessman who *has to* visit more customers per day than he can really manage. There is the woman who is trying to fit the school run in with her job and her shopping. These people have pressures coming from the culture of the 1990s, but they are also just inflicting it upon themselves. I have even seen a *nun* complaining of not having enough hours in the day to do everything that she felt was required of her!

Some psychologists have called this The Treadmill Syndrome (29), and see it as a sad reflection on modern times. People are working longer and longer hours to fulfil the demands of the job, as well as to pay their increasingly high mortgages. But working longer hours produces further costs, such as a need for labour-saving household equipment, convenience foods, domestic help, childcare, and two cars. These may be paid for by using credit cards and a permanent state of debt. Hence there is no escape from this treadmill, and they keep up the pace in the hope that they will never become exhausted.

There used to be light at the end of the tunnel for parents struggling to cope with the costs of a growing family. One day the children would grow up and become financially independent. They might even contribute to the family income. But now there is a danger that they will continue to require support during more and more years of education. And at the same time these young people may have developed unrealistic expectations of a high standard of living.

People on this treadmill are at risk of physical and emotional exhaustion, and consequent ill-health. They need to review their use of the words Have To. There is usually more scope than they realise to assert themselves against demands, and to adopt a gentler pace of life.

16th September 1997.

The Thatcher government has gone. There is an audible sigh of relief, but also uncertainty about whether we will have to go through a continuing series of managerial changes, reversing the previous changes.

At least the palmtops have gone. No more tedious lists of patients to fill in at the end of every day. We have been doing that for years, and actually I feel a little uneasy now about not doing it. I used to have a bit of a fantasy that some manager at headquarters looked at my data and took an interest in what I was doing. In reality, of course, it merely went on to the computer and got absorbed into loads of other data. But now I cannot pretend any more. Management really does not have any interest in my work.

I am continuing to work just the same, however. There is a never ending supply of people to be seen. And I seem to be working later and later in the evenings, to fit in with patients who work during the day. However, I always take Friday afternoons off as a reward.

12th August 1998.

I can't help noticing that fewer patients have been referred recently, and from only a limited number of GP practices. It is still quite enough, and indeed it means that I can give more sessions to each patient, and hopefully do better quality work. But I am wondering what is going on. Have I offended some of the GPs, or made some mistakes? Are they sending their patients somewhere else? I really don't know, but I am wary of asking, as I don't want to trigger off a renewed wave of excessive referrals.

Perhaps they are referring more to the Psychiatrists again, now that the old guard has gone and been replaced with fresh faces. Or perhaps the *growth of Counselling* is no longer a myth and is beginning to take some of the workload. As well as the Community Psychiatric Nurses who do some counselling in the GP practices, there are increasing numbers of assorted Counsellors available privately (and possibly developing links with the NHS).

Some psychologists are a bit dubious about Counsellors, and suggest that their qualifications and professionalism are not up to scratch. This reminds me of the things that the Psychiatrists used to say about Psychologists, which is a bit ironic. I am more inclined to support these newcomers (as long as they are not obviously mad or bad, of course). After all, the important aim here is to provide therapy for all the patients who would benefit from it, and psychologists are never going to be numerous enough to do the job.

9th June 1999.

I wonder if it is time for me to reinvigorate my work. It is about fifteen years now since I campaigned for Primary Care services and independence from psychiatry. Those battles were so bitter that I was then forced to isolate myself from the psychiatrists and their hospitals. I wish I could have remained on friendly terms, as in the early years.

Consequently I have lost touch with the kind of services that are being provided by psychiatrists and others such as the community nurses. I don't even know what is going on in the psychology department at the hospital. For many years I have assumed that I had moved on and left these others behind. But perhaps things have changed, and now I am the one in danger of missing the boat.

Am I continuing to fight old battles that have long been won? No one questions now that there are thousands and thousands of people who need help, and that psychological or talking therapies can help them. No one questions that this help can be given by a variety of professionals, including psychologists, psychiatrists, nurses, and counsellors. And that they should be readily accessible through the Primary Care system. The only question is over the lack of resources to supply this need.

I am now very senior in my career and being paid a top salary, but I seem to be doing less and less to earn it. This makes me feel rather guilty, but also vulnerable, as it renders me vulnerable to attack by any manager looking at value for money. I am only safe at the moment because the managers are too busy once more coming to terms with the new government.

I have decided to make a pre-emptive strike, by sending management a report about all this, offering to be reorganised to fit in with the improved mental health services that are being planned for the new century.

25th January 2000.

There has been no reply to my letter. I hate this managerial habit of not replying to anything that they don't know what to do with. If they just replied and explained that they needed time to consider it, I would probably wait patiently for another year. But silence means that there is no chance of anything happening in the foreseeable future. I cannot hang about any longer. I have decided to retire.

There was a time when I would have fought on, but not now. Been there, done that. I cannot be bothered. Should I diagnose myself as suffering from *burnout,* perhaps? Well, maybe, sort of. It is difficult to see yourself as others might see you, so I am not sure. I just feel that I have been doing what I do for a long time (30 years), virtually non-stop, and I have had enough. That is not a completely bad feeling, as it includes the idea that I am satisfied and my job is done.

The particular light that has gone out is my *fascination with listening.* All my life I have paid great attention to anything that I can hear, greater even than visual experiences. Hobbies such as playing the violin (where you have to listen very carefully to the notes you are producing) and short wave radio (where you have to strain to hear some distant broadcast) were simply exercises for my ears. But further than that, I was always alert for *the things that people say, and what they mean by them.* This made me a very good pupil at school, where no teacher ever had to tell me to *pay attention.*

In the light of this, it is entirely natural that I became a clinical psychologist. I am one of those people who can listen to someone else with great interest, observing what they say and what they mean, and doing so without any urge to interrupt them every few minutes. Afterwards, I can remember exactly what they said (not some garbled version of it), and exactly who said it.

There is always a danger of taking words too seriously, of course, forgetting that people tell lies, get things wrong, and generally talk rubbish. Is this why I have been so irritated and demoralised by the culture of Management Speak? Do other people simply *not listen* to it?

I was always fascinated by listening to patients' stories. Each patient was different, no matter how many thousands I had seen. There was always something new to learn. But now I just feel I have heard it all before. Maybe this is true, but I doubt it. My light has gone out.

Burnout is defined as a syndrome with three aspects. Emotional Exhaustion includes feelings of being emotionally overextended and depleted. Depersonalisation or Cynicism is a negative, callous or excessively detached response to patients. Reduced Personal Accomplishment includes feelings of lack of achievement and productivity at work.

One survey (30) of clinical psychologists in the UK found that significant numbers of them were burnt out, as measured by questionnaires. Nearly half of those surveyed indicated a high likelihood of leaving their job. A proportion of those who are burnt out may be providing a poor quality of care to their patients. This has implications for the psychologists, their patients, the profession and the NHS.

Burnout can be suffered by younger therapists, not just those with long service. It is a response to the chronic emotional strain of dealing extensively with other human beings who are troubled or in distress (31).

More awareness of the problem might encourage the greater use of strategies to counteract it. There are a number of possible strategies which, together, may help to prevent burnout. For example, having a mentor or supervisor to whom you can turn for discussion or advice. Belonging to a professional organisation. Keeping your paperwork in good order. Keeping up to date with your profession. Taking regular time off. On the personal front, developing outside interests or hobbies. Getting involved with your local community. Meeting people other than psychologists. Turning off the therapeutic mode with your friends and family. Trying to achieve a balance between work, intimate relationships, parenthood, community, friends and solitude.

23rd March 2000.

I have handed in my resignation, giving three months notice. Strangely enough, after all my moaning about managers, I now find that I don't actually have one. With all the reshuffling that has gone on, they seem to have forgotten about me. So I gave my resignation to the personnel manager. Already I am beginning to feel detached from the sound and fury of the NHS.

There have been many writings about the political and managerial state of the NHS. One clinical psychologist (32) wrote that despite the election of a Labour government, there remains a climate of computerisation, competition and fear, mirroring the desperation of a war-zone street market. This is a challenge for health service policy-makers. Quite simply, the government of the day needs to achieve an alliance with the people who work for the NHS. This will only happen if policies make sense, if their implementation is humane, and if people are treated as people and not as business assets. The well being of public service employees would be enhanced by a variety of environmental and personal factors, such as a sense of belonging, a reasonable degree of trust, and an assurance of continuing employment. The government really does not need to continually meddle to keep us under control. We are mostly too busy to plan a revolution yet.

All of the other professions in the NHS have had problems.

During the 1990s it was noted (33) that there had been a rise in the number of psychiatrists retiring early, and a worrying number of posts were being left unfilled. A survey revealed multiple reasons being given for early retirement, but the biggest one was the increasing bureaucracy and paperwork.

There is little evidence that psychiatrists no longer enjoy psychiatry. In fact many who retire early go on to do private practice. Most psychiatrists regard their out-patient clinic as the last refuge of sanity in the week's work. The doctor-patient relationship reminds them of why they chose to do psychiatry in the first place.

When people ask me why I am retiring, I don't mention all this stuff about management. If they don't work in the NHS, they don't understand it, and if they do work for the NHS they know all about it. What I tell them is that I have been working with patients for 30 years, and my life has been ruled by my appointments diary for all of that time. During those 30 years, I once managed to have two consecutive weeks off, but otherwise I took most of my holiday allowance in the form of long weekends.

Any greater absence would lead to a pile of work on my return, and longer hours of work to catch up. I am now joking that the only way I can get some time off is to retire! But no one laughs.

30th June 2000.

I saw my last patient earlier this week. *Saw my last patient!* My colleagues cannot believe that I am not sad about this. Instead, I feel a weight off my shoulders, and some rising excitement. It is a new millennium, and I am celebrating with a new car, a new house, and time to myself.

POSTSCRIPT 2010

I have been trying to take no interest in the NHS and its mental health services. Instead, I have been amusing myself by writing a little self-help book (34) about protecting yourself from people with stressfully irritating personalities. Perhaps I could have used this if I had still been working?

Then one day I was browsing the newspapers (as we retired people do), and was amazed to read about someone called Lord Layard, who had published a report urging that psychological therapy should be made available to everyone in Britain who requires it. Apparently Layard is a distinguished economist, and his report argued that such a service would pay for itself by reducing the expenditure on social security benefits that are paid to people unable to go to work because of anxiety and depression. He estimated that a person off sick costs the taxpayer £750 every month, while a course of therapy only costs £750 and would save at least a month on benefits.

My first reaction was to laugh. Would anyone would take any notice of an economist talking about psychology? The psychology profession has tried the economic argument in the past, but it has not impressed anyone. However, apparently Layard has considerable influence in government circles and his arguments have been accepted.

This has led to a number of government-funded initiatives, known as the Increasing Access to Psychological Therapies (IAPT) programme (35). It is focussed at present on adults with common mental health problems, and cognitive behavioural therapy is the main recommended treatment. There is recognition of the value of either *low intensity treatment* (just four sessions of simple techniques), or *high intensity treatment* (longer and more highly skilled), according to the individual client's need.

The programme has already started in some pilot areas, together with training programmes for a new wave of psychological therapists (not necessarily psychologists). This has injected much needed finance into the chronically under-funded adult mental health services.

The IAPT programme has been given a somewhat cautious welcome by the psychology profession. *There are a lot of good things about it, but ...* seems to be the general feeling. This may well be a wise stance to take, but why is no one expressing their delight at this amazing recognition of the value of psychological therapy? Perhaps it is only older psychologists such as myself who remember when we were only grudgingly allowed to try a bit of therapy, even though we were better qualified than those who were standing in our way. We were pioneers at a time when there were at most two psychologists in an entire county (and sometimes none at all). Access to therapy was virtually non-existent, but no one saw its value anyway. Things have changed a great deal in 40 years, but Improving Access is still crucial.

Critics of Layard have pointed to a number of flaws (36). It is uncertain whether the economic benefits would flow quite as easily as suggested. A lot of people may be ill because of social and economic reasons which are not fixable by therapy. When the dust has settled and it is realised that cognitive behavioural therapy is not the panacea it has been made out to be, there could be a backlash against all psychological therapies.

There is professional unease at the idea of therapy being a routine application of particular methods or techniques that can somehow deliver happy, adjusted people at low cost. The reality is that it is a skilled and often certain endeavour that demands a high level of interpersonal skills and a particular expertise. This is as true of cognitive behavioural therapy as of any other brand.

I can understand psychologists getting into a sweat about the idea of simple therapies being given by therapists with only elementary skills, as if the whole process of therapy is being required to *dumb down*. Psychiatrists too have been standing up recently (37) to declare pride in their profession and its areas of expertise, which have been eroded by clinical psychologists and others. But I think there is more to psychology than trying to be clever.

My experience in Primary Care taught me the value of simple ideas and simple therapies. Many people are helped (and self-helped) by such approaches, and really don't need great expertise. If IAPT can produce more therapists for this task, we should welcome all the help we can get. No doubt there will be snags and failures, and it will take a lot longer than planned to get it right, but it will be an interesting journey.

The newspapers have been reporting teething problems in the roll-out of the IAPT programme. Insufficient numbers of therapists have been trained, not enough patients have come off benefits, and people are failing to use the help line. There may be some threat to the funding of the programme, especially in the current economic recession.

In the meantime, clinical psychologists need to become very clear about their core identity, which does distinguish them from any other profession, whatever overlaps there might be. David Smail (38) expressed this very well, as follows:

Clinical psychology has always been about invention and discovery, critique and empirical investigation. We need to further develop the empirical critique of therapy and counselling, we must continue to question the shortcomings of the illness model, and we must strive to understand our patients in a way that is both accurate and open to investigation. Our function is not just to deliver pre-identified packages of care, but to foster the skills of invention, hypothesis-testing and evaluation, which are possessed by very few others in the field.

Some would say that these are not clinical, but academic functions. I do not think so. Real knowledge can only be gained and elaborated by staying in the traditional scientist-practitioner role, and perhaps we need to be a bit bolder about saying so.

REFERENCES

(1) Cheshire, K. and Pilgrim, D. (2004). A Short Introduction to Clinical Psychology. London: Sage Publications.

(2) Jones, K. (1998). Mental Health and Social Policy, 1845-1959. London: Routledge.

(3) Eysenck, H. J. (1962). Sense and Nonsense in Psychology. London: Penguin.

(4) Shapiro, D. (2002). Renewing the scientist-practitioner model. The Psychologist, 15, 5, 232-234.

(5) Ingram, A. ed. (1998). Patterns of Madness in the Eighteenth Century. Liverpool University Press.

(6) Eysenck, M. W. (1994). Individual Differences: Normal and Abnormal. London: Psychology Press.

(7) Robb, B. (1967). Sans Everything: A Case to Answer. London: Nelson.

(8) Report of Committee of Enquiry (1976). St. Augustine's Hospital, Chartham, Canterbury. South East Thames Area Health Authority.

(9) Hall, P. and Gillard, R. (1982). The Worcester Development Project. International Journal of Social Psychiatry, 28, 3, 163-172.

(10) Sandison, R. (2000). A Century of Psychiatry, Psychotherapy and Group Analysis. London: Jessica Kingsley.

(11) Smith, A. (1975). Secret Lie Detector in the Lab. New Scientist, 28th August, 476-478.

(12) Dean-Davis, R. (2009). The Wars of Rosie. London: Pennant Books.

(13) Hall, P., Smith, G. A., Husain, B. and Treadwell, E. A. (1979). Voice speed in depression. IRCS Medical Science, 7,111.

(14) Smith, G. A. (1977). Voice analysis for the measurement of anxiety. British Journal of Medical Psychology, 50, 367-373.

(15) Tombs, D. and Bennett, C. (1987). The Evaluation of the Worcester Development Project. International Journal of Social Psychiatry, 33, 2, 92-98.

(16) Department of Health and Social Security (1977). The Role of Psychologists in the Health Service. London: HMSO.

(17) Haslam, M. T. (1981). Obstacles and rivals. Psychiatric Bulletin, 5, 148.

(18) Wilson, S. (2002). Survey of the use of abreaction by consultant psychiatrists. Psychiatric Bulletin, 26, 58-60.

(19) Horrocks, P. (1986). The role of the Health Advisory Service in psychiatry. Psychiatric Bulletin, 10, 145-146.

(20) Bussey, A. (1984). Professional advice to the National Health Service - the medium or the message? British Medical Journal, 289, 204-206

(21) NHS Management Enquiry Report (1983). London: DHSS.

(22) Mental Health Foundation report (2008). While we are Waiting.

(23) Smith, G. A. (1988). Caffeine reduction as an adjunct to anxiety management. British Journal of Clinical Psychology, 27, 265-266.

(24) Kennedy, P. and Llewelyn, S. (2001). Does the future belong to the scientist-practitioner? The Psychologist, 14, 2, 74-78.

(25) Department of Health report (1989). Working for Patients. London: HMSO.

(26) Murdock, A., Rodgers, C., Lindsay, H. and Tham, T. C. K. (2002). Why do patients not keep their appointments? Journal of the Royal Society of Medicine, 95, 284-286.

(27) Obituary. Professor Sir William Trethowan (1996) Psychiatric Bulletin, 20, 573-575.

(28) Mayou, R., Bryant, B. and Duthie, R. (1993). Psychiatric consequences of road traffic accidents. British Medical Journal, 307, 647-651.

(29) Hudson-Allez, G. (1999). The treadmill syndrome. The Psychologist, 12, 11, 548-549.

(30) Mehta, R. (2007). Burnout of Clinical Psychologists in the UK. Available from: http://www.lancs.ac.uk/shm/dhr/research/mental/burnout ofcps.htm

(31) Maslach, C. (1982). Burnout - the Cost of Caring. Englewood Cliffs, NJ: Prentice Hall.

(32) Newnes, C. (2001). Government policy and the people who work for the NHS. Clinical Psychology Forum, 7, 46-50.

(33) Kendell, R. E. and Pearce, A. (1997). Consultant psychiatrists who retired prematurely in 1995 and 1996. Psychiatric Bulletin, 21, 741-745.

(34) Smith, G. A. (2007). Who's your Problem? Pest or Prat? Cambridge: Pegasus Elliot MacKenzie.

(35) Improving Access to Psychological Therapies (IAPT) programme (2006). Available from http://www.iapt.nhs.uk

(36) Marzillier, J. and Hall, J. (2009). The challenge of the Layard initiative. The Psychologist, 22, 5, 396-399.

(37) Craddock, N. et al (2008). Wake-up call for British psychiatry. The British Journal of Psychiatry, 193, 6-9.

(38) Smail, D. (1998). What's it all about? Clinical Psychology Forum, 119, 22-24.